ALFRED DELLER

A Singularity of Voice

Michael & Mollie Hardwick

PROTEUS
London & New York

For PEGGY
with fondest love

784.0924
H22a
118387
May 1981

PROTEUS BOOKS is an imprint of
The Proteus Publishing Group

United Kingdom
PROTEUS (PUBLISHING) LIMITED
Bremar House,
Sale Place,
London, W2 1PT.

United States
PROTEUS PUBLISHING CO., INC.
747 Third Avenue, 14th Floor,
New York, N.Y. 10017.

distributed by
CHARLES SCRIBNER'S SONS
597 Fifth Avenue,
New York, N.Y. 10017.

ISBN 0 906071 63 1

First published in U.K. September 1980.
First published in U.S. September 1980.
© 1980 by Michael and Mollie Hardwick.
All rights reserved.

Typeset in Hong Kong by
Pearl Island Filmsetters (H.K.) Ltd.
Printed in England

FOREWORD

by Sir Michael Tippett

This book tells a fascinating story, stretching as it does from a childhood which might almost be described as hang-over Dickensian (the authors even mention Gradgrind, though Dickens died forty-two years before Alfred Deller was born) to an international music career in the permissive society of the present time. Part of the fascination is the clear fact that Deller doesn't quite fit into either. He certainly didn't rule his family as his father ruled his mother and his siblings. But aspects of our present society disturbed him deeply, if we are to judge by his fulmination against beat groups. This all comes somehow, I think, from the integral quality of his Christianity. Gladys Keable speaks of this in the book: 'In bringing out the whole beauty of music he is bringing out something that is a beautiful part of life, and of the Trinity.' I can echo the first part of that sentence, but not the end; so that I have to make a special effort to imagine that if one felt the beauty of music in such terms then one might really feel 'convinced (with respect to beat music) that the whole question of dope-taking and juvenile delinquency is all linked up with this rotten influence'. This is surely the tremendous tradition of the arts as moral or immoral influences, which runs from Plato to the Puritans. It is hard to live by it nowadays.

The book is not merely a success story. Deller suffered more than most great artists from the negative sides of his genius: professional self-depreciation and insecurity; emotional depression. It is up to professional colleagues to help an artist with the former, as it is the burden of wife or friend to deal with the latter (Peggy Deller fully understands this). But Deller had to face extra problems and overcome peculiar susceptibilities owing to the very nature of his voice, And again it is ironical to note that present-day young people, hearing a lot of beat where voices are high or low quite irrespective of sex, and generally accepting our permissive society where virility is no longer a he-man mythology, must find Deller's worries about his voice, as he talks of them in this book, outside their ken.

Yet it is a success story; not only of a great singer, but of music itself—especially English music. For Deller was of the generation where Purcell and the Elizabethans have truly returned to find their public. Our musical forefathers worked hard to bring this about, as we have worked hard. But the moment was not ripe for them, while we have seen the flowering. It was always known to history books that *Music for a While* was in its way as fine as 'Dido's Lament'. But the public only knew this, or was even willing to know this, through Deller's first recording. In the same way it is Deller's generation that first carried English music abroad, to an at last relatively unprejudiced foreign public. To Germany, Purcell, and to a lesser degree the Elizabethans, was as much a revelation as, say, Monteverdi was to us. It was also the same in America. For just because we accept as automatic that the roots of American literature are English, we find it sometimes difficult to realize that the roots of American concert music are German. (Jazz is, of course, not German at all: but Deller does not belong to that story.) So that until the prejudice and falsity of the older notions of the non-musicality of our country gave over, there was little to be done. Now, it is safe to say, that has all changed and Deller was one of England's most successful artists over the whole of that vast land.

I have stressed the more impersonal aspects of Deller's success story because this is where his true immortality must rest. Not so much because such an artist issued from such an apparently unpropitious family, or that he had to wait so many years to find his own means to maturity and fulfilment, but because he was a particular and special musician among the select group of internationally esteemed performers, and in his field unique.

INTRODUCTION

Music,
Music for a while
Shall all your cares beguile.

Alfred Deller was more than a singer: he was a musical experience. As with many new experiences, there was some shock on first hearing him, when, from that great frame and manly presence, there issued those flute-like sounds, ranging the register of the female alto, yet unmistakably masculine in character. He and those who first promoted him in public recognized this reaction as something which he had to accept and to fight his audiences for: 'I have trained myself not to be upset by it, and I only hope that the audience will quickly get over this natural surprise and settle down to listen to the voice as a musical instrument. Thank heaven, most people do.'

What they heard was something unique, not in the sense of freak, but a consummate artistry and emotional instinct, expressed in a long-lost voice type intimately associated with the golden age of English music of the sixteenth and seventeenth centuries, driven into obscurity with that music by eighteenth century Italianism and nineteenth century romanticism, and resurrected unwittingly by the self-taught Alfred Deller in our own time. It is as though an amateur archaeologist had stumbled upon a treasure of infinite value and found he possessed the gifts and perception to make himself the world's leading authority on it.

Listening to Deller is to tune in directly to those times of Dowland, Campion and then Purcell, whose perfection is instantly recognizable and is especially acceptable to a new generation who do not care to wallow in sticky romanticism but find the engineered music of our time unable to fulfil that emotional function which is music's chief *raison d'être*. The music in which Alfred Deller mainly dealt proves to be of timeless vitality, and, especially in the case of Dowland, surprisingly modern idiom. It is the kind of antique one chooses to live with, rather than relegate to a cabinet.

A great fascination of Alfred's story is to watch it taking shape from the most inauspicious of beginnings, moving from phase to phase with a smoothness which most of us envy. Again and again we see the cue given and perfectly accepted: the apparent chance circumstance producing a significant outcome; the seemingly unremarkable encounter leading to a relationship of major importance in his life or art. There is something of predestination about it; he himself had no doubt about that.

Uniquely gifted, he was led by his art along a path lonelier than he might have chosen to tread. Worldwide renown cost him much of the home life he valued and kept him a constant traveller, which he disliked. Peggy, the wife and helpmeet to whom he owed so much, saw far less of him than when he was unknown: in her words, 'It had to be the one way or the other—and the other would never have satisfied him.'

Paradoxically, the country whose greatest music he helped achieve universal respect for saw least of him. For two-thirds of every year he was abroad, singing to packed and ever-appreciative audiences throughout Europe, the Americas, Australasia and the East. It was a great regret to him that England had paid less heed to him after his unexpected emergence than it might have done, so that his performing links overseas largely took over his career. For all his work's influence upon the foreign view of our artistic capacity the only national honour bestowed on him was a belated and inadequate O.B.E. in 1970. Other awards, all in his later years, were a Doctorate of Letters from the

University of Kent at Canterbury, a Doctorate of Music from the University of Leicester, Honorary Membership of the Royal Academy of Music, London; and, especially pleasing to him, the Edward Hardy medal for services to his native county, Kent.

As we have remarked in the book, he sought no advancement through cliques and contrived relationships. He employed no publicists, indulged in no attention-catching lifestyle. He missed many opportunities in consequence, but there was enough left over to fulfil him. Though he regretted some things he could not have, or had had and lost, he was conscious above all of standing at the very centre of his true circle, a man born and destined to do what he was doing, humbly aware of the God-given privilege this implied. Someone said that everything he did was an act of worship, and he would have been the last to deny that.

On the metaphysical plane, believers in reincarnation would have little difficulty in making out a case based on him. There was more of the Tudor to him than that beard: an un-modern blend of artistic sensibility, mystical preoccupation, brooding melancholy, yet infectious gaiety. 'In that moment, the centuries rolled back,' Michael Tippett recalls of first hearing Deller sing. Millions of others have shared that experience by now, and will go on doing so through his many recordings. It was no artistic façade. To know him, to work with him, to eat and drink and talk and joke with him, left that impression still intact.

In making this revised and expanded version of our original biography, published a decade before his death, we have used much material which remains valid and renew our thanks to the many family members, colleagues, friends and others who gave us their comments and recollections. Like theirs, new contributions are attributed in the text, and we express our general thanks.

The letters in Chapter Ten are reproduced by kind permission of the late Lord Britten and Sir Peter Pears. We thank again Sir Michael Tippett for his Foreword and other help. We are deeply grateful to John Ward, R.A., for allowing us free use of illustrations, and to Alan Howlett for letting us include his complete discography. No acknowledgment would be complete without the names of Peggy Deller and her son Mark, for their frank and vigorous co-operation in up-dating this story.

Our royalties from this book are being given over to the Alfred Deller Memorial Trust, whose aims are to provide a memorial window to him at All Saints Church, Boughton Aluph, Kent, and to endow a Scholarship at the Royal Northern College of Music, Manchester, for students of early music, with particular reference to the countertenor voice.

MICHAEL AND MOLLIE HARDWICK, 1980

ONE

The name once meant 'Dweller in the dell'. Robert atte Delle lived in Sussex in 1296, and there were families elsewhere named Dellere, Dellar, Delleman and Dell. There may be Flemish associations and some connection with Huguenot settlers in this country.

For one whose character and art and even appearance might seem to be in the nature of a throwback to the late Middle Ages, Alfred Deller was surprisingly unconcerned about his origins. He did not know his grandparents on either side, and was never much moved to enquire about them. All he did know was that his father's family lived in Hertfordshire and is not related to the only other sizeable Deller clan in England still, whose cafés have been refreshing West Country folk for many years.

His father, Thomas William Deller, was born in Ware, Hertfordshire, on 7 February 1872, the son of a doctor's coachman who contracted smallpox from one of his employer's patients and died of it, aged twenty-one. He left a widow, who married again twice, a daughter, and the one son, William, who left school at twelve and went to work on the land. In those days of Hiring Fairs, at which agricultural employers took on their labour for the coming year, a familiar sight was a resplendent recruiting sergeant, seated with his drummer outside an inn, and, with beer and eloquence, cajoling young men into accepting the Queen's Shilling. One of these martial evangelists so moved young William Deller's spirit that he offered to testify in the appropriate way. The sergeant laughed and told him to stay on the land and grow up a little before trying again.

When he was fourteen, armed with a recommendation

of character, he left the village for London, where he stayed with an uncle and aunt and began an apprenticeship as fireman's assistant on the railway. The honourable and not unexciting career of engine driver lay ahead of him if he had persevered; but he gave up one form of transport for another, becoming a horse omnibus driver. A natural instinct for handling horses enabled him to manage with ease the teams of four or six in London's congested streets, and when, one day, a lead horse went mad and threatened to send the whole team berserk he knew just what to do. Crawling over the backs of the plunging beasts, he cut the demented one's throat—or so an unlikely family legend insists.

The memory of the recruiting sergeant lingered in his mind, however, and he determined to try again. Giving a false age, he managed to enlist into the 18th Hussars.

William Deller was made for the army, and the army for him. He loved everything about it; even the harsh discipline of those times. He excelled as a horseman. When his regiment moved to India he was able to distinguish himself at tent-pegging and the other horseback sports of that station. He began also to take an interest in physical training, for which he discovered a natural bent. Passing the necessary examinations, he was made an instructor, with sergeant's rank.

In 1895 the regiment returned from India. Walking out in London, Sergeant Deller met a nurse, Mary Cave, who worked at the Consumptive Hospital, Brompton, and lived with a sister in Mare Street, Hackney. She was small, placid and pretty, with shining black hair and merry, dark sloe eyes; he was imperial, perfectly proportioned, his ramrod carriage adding illusory inches to his medium height. They made a striking couple, and they loved one another. They were married before the bugle and drum summoned Sergeant Deller away to South Africa to fight the Boers.

When the regiment returned from the war in 1902, Mary took rooms for herself and baby Emma opposite the barracks in Canterbury and William contrived to spend much of his time with them in this first family home. But Canterbury lies in a hill-encircled hollow through which runs the River Stour. Its vaporous atmosphere began to affect the baby, who had always been 'chesty'. When the doctor recommended Mary to move to some healthier place, William, rather than be parted from his wife and child again, sought and obtained his discharge from the colours, in 1903.

He was tremendously fit, and could have had many more years of useful and enjoyable service. The army and his family were all that mattered to him in life. He gave up the former for the latter, and spent the rest of his days regretting it.

They moved only a few miles from Canterbury, to Margate, more fashionable then than now and re-nowned for its bracing seaside air. At their little house in Northdown Road Sergeant Deller, as he continued to be known, set up in the insecure practice of freelance physical training instructor. For a time he had a partner, Major Hayes, one of his former regimental officers; but the major withdrew after a few months and a brass plate was screwed on to the Dellers' front gate-post, reading 'Sergeant T.W. Deller, Swedish exercises, gym-nastics'.

Margate and the Thanet coast have long been favoured sites for boys' and girls' colleges, and the Sergeant was soon busy building up a connection with as many of them as would engage him, bicycling from one to another to take an hour's physical jerks, a boxing lesson, a fencing class. The trim, taut figure, the cropped military haircut and perfectly disciplined moustache, the snow-white, unwrinkled drill vest bearing the crown and crossed cutlasses of the army physical train-ing instructor, the smart cummerbund and razor-creased trousers: the combination of precisions which made up Sergeant Deller was soon a familiar and respected sight throughout the Thanet towns.

Even so, life was precarious for the Dellers. The

Sergeant's work paid him well in terms of continued physical fitness, but in no other sense. His fees were necessarily low, yet slow in the payment, for the schools which employed him sent parents their bills term by term and had themselves to wait long periods for settlement. Sergeant Deller did not get his share until every parent had paid up and his account could be settled complete. His tiny capital, augmented by a meagre income from private classes, had to carry the family economy meanwhile. They practised every possible economy, paying for nothing they could manage to do for themselves. The Sergeant, fortunately a gifted gardener, worked an allotment to grow the bulk of their food. He kept hens. He did all the shoe repairs in what he called his 'snobbing shop' in the garden shed. He swept the chimneys and undertook every kind of household make and mend. The school holidays, when he faced weeks of semi-idleness, were the worst times. Then, in addition to his customary early morning run or walk, he would spend the empty afternoons running by the hour, whatever the weather, returning flushed, but breathing as easily as when he had set out, for a soak in a hot bath and a rub down with liniment. He had always energy and to spare, but opportunities for earning a living by it were not his to make.

Mary gave her full share. If a few pence could be saved at the cost of an hour's hard work, saved they were. One of her children retained a vivid memory of coming home from school on winter afternoons, to find the kitchen dense with steam and his little mother, her pretty face scarlet and her hair saturated, pounding the clothes which boiled in the copper. She found time off from this incessant toil to bear seven children, four boys and three girls, in addition to having at least two miscarriages. When they were old enough to be useful the children helped with household tasks; but only those requiring minimum skill. With three daughters willing to relieve her, Mary never relinquished the cookery. She could not: there had never been time to teach any of the girls how to do it.

It was the Sergeant, with his tidy, military mind, who kept them from poverty, A less organized household might well have disintegrated into hopelessness and chaos. He appreciated each domestic problem as it arose, promptly taking the appropriate action to deal with it, Untidy situations were as distasteful to him as unpunctuality or disobedience. Unfortunately for his gentle, uncomplaining little wife and their children, his virtues gave birth to his vice. The self-discipline which would remain his lifelong creed was reflected in the relentless routine and code of behaviour which he imposed upon his family.

William Deller neither would, nor could, make adjustment or concession to civilian life. Mentally, as well as nominally, he remained the Sergeant, outranked by no one in his household. In drilling classes of children he still felt the uplift of authority which he was not prepared to relinquish amongst his own family. Everything would be done the way he wanted it, or he would know the reason why. At the best of times his voice was loud and his tone hectoring. If crossed in the slightest way he would lose his temper in a flash. When he was really aggrieved, his rage took physical form.

The children were sometimes allowed to go to see a silent film. Occasionally there would be no seats available at the afternoon performance in the tiny cinema, so they were permitted to go to the evening show, on condition that they were home by some strictly set time. Now and then, the fascination of the film would make them oblivious to the fact that the performance was over-running by a few minutes. Emerging at last, horrified to see the clock, they would run all the way home, arriving near to collapse but still a minute or two late. They knew what they would find: the Sergeant, watch in one hand, long black razor strop from the hook near the bathroom door in the other. Neither excuse nor apology could move him, as neither excuse nor apology could have saved any soldier running late on to the parade ground. The beatings he gave them were violent, sometimes close to savage. Mary Deller knew better than to intervene. One of her daughters remembered her standing as near to the child being punished as she dared, holding it, if she could, in reassurance, but never remonstrating with her husband. 'One's enough, Em,' she whispered once; and Emma knew that the blows she was receiving would have been turned upon her mother if she had spoken out.

There were many rules to infringe. Talking at table was not allowed, and no one might rise until final Grace had been said. Newspapers and magazines were forbidden in the house. Absolute punctuality on every occasion was mandatory, and the summons of the Sergeant's piercing whistle had to be obeyed instantly by everyone within earshot.

Yet there was no insistence on early rising or physical jerks before breakfast. The Sergeant's outbursts were feared and resented, but his disciplinary demands were accepted as reasonable. He could be the kindest, most considerate of men, spending long hours in anxious attendance on any of them who fell sick. For all her apparent meekness and refusal to oppose him, Mary quietly ruled her Sergeant. He loved her intensely and relied upon her more than he knew. The worst times of all were when he would turn on her, and the children would tremble to hear his shouting from behind the closed bedroom door. Unreasoning jealousy brought out the worst in him. The most monstrous act of injustice followed Emma's return from her honeymoon. She only learned later that after she and her husband had departed the Sergeant had turned on Mary in a frenzy of abuse and accusation, and all because she had allowed Emma's husband to kiss her good-bye. Thereafter, whenever Mary went to answer the door to a tradesman the Sergeant would contrive to hover in the background, just to make sure that she was not 'carrying on' again.

Em herself had earlier found an effective way of

dealing with one of her father's outbursts. Hearing him beating her brother Tom, she shouted, 'If you don't damn well stop hitting him, Dad, I'm going to fetch a policeman.' The threat, she knew, would have no effect; the oath would. The beating ceased at once. The Sergeant thundered down the stairs after Em, who wisely ran into the main street, aware that even uncontrollable temper could not make her father behave in an undignified way before strangers. Managing to give him the slip, she walked about for a time, hoping his temper would cool, before returning home and sneaking quietly into the kitchen, where her mother was nursing the latest baby. 'Mum,' she whispered, 'give me the baby to hold, then Dad won't be able to hit me.'

The baby she clutched in self-protection when the Sergeant entered was Alfred Deller.

He had been born on 31 May 1912, the youngest of the four boys. Alfred George Deller became known at once to the family as Young Alf.

By this time the family's finances were in a healthier state. Over the years the Sergeant's connections had snowballed. He now went further afield to take his classes, and close to the new home to which they soon moved in Arthur Road, Margate, there was a church hall which he was able to rent and use as a gymnasium. There was relative prosperity enough to make Alfred's childhood somewhat smoother and less restricted than that of his older brothers and sisters.

His first memory was of crying. He cried a great deal, at great length and very loudly. His worried mother decided to call the doctor. The doctor came, and Alfred cried for him. The doctor examined him, then turned to Mary with a laugh. 'No, Mrs Deller, there's nothing wrong with that boy. He has exceptional lungs, and he wants to exercise them. He cries for crying's sake.'

So Alfred was left to develop his lungs in the way Nature had arranged for him.

He was a good little boy, with a touch of seriousness from the beginning. He was a little spoilt, compared with the rest, though he felt his share of the black razor strop. Looking back on his father, he considered that his demands were no more unreasonable, and his punishments no more unjustified, than was customary in most families of their class. In the Deller household you knew just where you stood, what you could or could not do, and what would happen to you if you defaulted. Like army life, it carried its own kind of certainty and security. The Sergeant bullied, but he protected. He enforced rigid discipline, and led his family securely and unitedly through the difficulties of years of near-poverty. He spared nothing of himself, and took no selfish pleasures. He was as hard as his muscles, and as unbending with himself as with others. The gentle, sweet Mary deserved a man capable of more tenderness than he; but she loved him, knew precisely how to handle him and, as a parent, provided exactly the counter-influence to his in their children's up-bringing.

Having satisfied himself that all was proceeding tidily and smoothly according to his regulations, Sergeant William Deller could march off the parade ground into watchful ease. Much of his spare time was occupied with ledgers and accounts, but he had a favourite relaxation, reading army drill manuals, the contents of which, though he must have known them by heart, never lost their fascination for him. He would some-times instead read the Bible or Macaulay's *History of England*, both of which had accompanied him on his army travels, or, conscious of his lack of education, a dictionary. It was his boast that he had never read a novel. Like Mr Gradgrind, there was no room in his make-up for anything that was not unassailable, in-vulnerable fact. It was an attitude he shared with many of his generation, a Victorian equivalent of refusing to watch television 'on principle'.

Yet he had a keen sense of humour, even of fun. When he judged it the correct moment to do so, he would play on the floor with his children, his loud, barking voice drowning theirs and making the house ring with harsh noise. Mary unobtrusively covered her ears and, as at all times, made no complaint.

There was a small billiards table at which the Sergeant would play with his children. He bought a second-hand piano and let the girls have lessons. He played it himself, by ear, and bought himself a concertina, which he also contrived to master. Sometimes on Saturdays he would take Mary to music-hall at the Hippodrome, and their house windows often rattled to his bellowing of his favourite, 'Swing me up a little bit higher, Obadiah, do'.

One day, fulfilling a promise, the Sergeant returned home with a gramophone. Predictably, the records he bought with it were mostly of military marches, but there were some popular and sentimental songs, and another of his own favourites, 'The Laughing Policeman'. With the girls tinkling on the piano, the Sergeant, in good humour, roaring ditties to his own accordion accompaniment, and someone trying to listen to the gramophone, it was, in a cacophonous way, a musical household.

There is no substantial background of music, though. As in so many families, there are vague stories of talented great-aunts and uncles; inevitably, perhaps, from a time that had seen so much home music-making. The Sergeant's mother is said to have had a better-than-average voice, while Mary's brother Alfred could play the violin noticeably better than most amateurs. *

When he stopped crying for a moment Alfred Deller must have been aware of the music around him. When he resumed crying it was sometimes to demand to be

---

*The Austrian minor composer Johann Florian Deller (1729–73) is not known to have any link with the English family.

taken out to see 'the man with a stick on a piece of wood'. This turned out to be a street violinist whose appearance fascinated the child, though whether on account of his music, or the mechanics of the performance, nobody knows. But if Alfred Deller's musical inheritance was slight, and his father's contribution to it unmelodious, he acquired two things from the Sergeant which would prove to be amongst his chief assets as a singer, One of these was a massive physique, with a great chest enclosing splendid lungs. The other was the rhythmic sense which had always been one of his most valuable possessions.

'My father had an incredible sense of rhythm,' he recalled. 'From my youngest days I used to go and watch him taking classes of twenty or thirty boys, swinging the Indian clubs while someone played the old piano in the corner of the gym. Father's sense of timing was faultless, and he would have the whole thing moving as precisely as a machine. It was the same when he exercised on the horizontal bars and the rings. He would swing and twist and somersault in perfect time. The rhythmic sense is, of course, as fundamental to music as it is to gymnastics, and I have always believed that I learnt the essentials of rhythm in my father's gym.'

When war came, two years after Alfred Deller's birth, the family suffered a severe setback. The Sergeant bore the first, cruellest shock of it when he hastened to enlist, and was rejected on the grounds of age. He was forty-two but fitter than most younger men and capable of playing an important part in their training. The best he could manage was to engage in recruiting, for which he was not given uniform to put on. One of the bitterest experiences of his life was being sneered at by strangers who, noting his trim figure, believed him to be a much younger man who had shirked active service.

The psychological blow to a man for whom the army was life itself, yet who could only stand helplessly on the sidelines of the war, was considerable. Even harsher, in practical terms, was the blow the war struck to his livelihood. Zeppelins appeared over Thanet in 1916, followed in 1917 by German bombers. Margate was shelled from the sea. Many boarding schools hastily closed their premises and moved to less vulnerable places, leaving the Sergeant with barely a handful of pupils. The connections he had built up were severed, with nothing to substitute for them. There was only one thing for him to do: he had to follow his pupils. Several of his schools had set up again in the Brighton areas, so for months he travelled by train every day from Margate to Brighton, a journey of about a hundred miles, and back.

At their home in Arthur Road the family carried on, sitting out the air-raid warnings in their large coal cellar, which the Sergeant had equipped with benches. With money scarcer than ever, and six children on her hands, Mary worked even harder than before. When she did find time to relax, she built houses for them out of kindling wood and sometimes read to them. Her taste was for the romantic and sentimental: Harrison Ainsworth's historical romances of old London, Dickens in his more melting moments, tear-provoking stories by Victorian ladies about orphans in the storm. Most of all, she loved to read the serial stories from newspapers and magazines which, in the Sergeant's absence, she could enjoy in safety.

In time, even the Sergeant's stamina began to wilt under the strain of so much travelling. He closed the Margate home, taking his family to live with him at a house in Hove, where he could be near his pupils and use the saved time by taking on still more. It was there that Young Alf, then aged four, first went to school and, soon after, appeared before an audience for the first time. Dressed in a sailor suit, he took part in a school concert, dancing a hornpipe and singing. It was a minor milestone indeed in his career, but one he remembered often when he performed fifty and more years later:

'There was no sort of stage or dressing room, of course. We just performed on the classroom floor, and before it was our turn to come on we crouched down behind the old upright piano. I can still smell the dusty green cloth backing to the piano, as I waited there with the butterflies fluttering in my stomach. It was the same nervous feeling that one gets before any kind of performance, and that musty smell comes back to me often today, when I'm waiting to go on.'

After the Armistice the family returned to Margate. The evacuated schools re-opened, and Sergeant Deller was once more in demand. The war years had hit him hard, but had not changed him. He was still fussing over untidiness or supposed slovenliness, and meting out the regulation punishment for the graver breaches of discipline, though not without opposition now from the older children. He had lost nothing of his energy or appearance. Every day he would weigh and measure himself. 'That tape-measure!' Mary murmured to a visitor, out of his hearing. But she understood his preoccupation. His physique and stamina were his only assets as a bread-winner. They repaid the close attention he gave them by providing the living. If he were to lose them, he and the family would be finished.

The family was now complete, from the oldest daughter, Emma, to Tom, Rose, Len, Horace, Alf and Grace. The older children were now able to look after the younger. Fortunately, they all got on well together. Alfred found himself mostly in the care of his brother Horace, five years his senior. Like all the Deller boys they were fond of games, particularly football and cricket, and their good physique made them more than competent players. Horace and he would spend hours in a field practising diving catches with a cricket ball, or bowling to each other using wickets chalked on a wall. ('When Alf sent down a fast one there was a touch of the Larwood about him,' another former player recalls.)

Horace was an ardent entrant in newspaper competitions. One year the *Daily Mail* organised a summer seaside competition featuring their children's cartoon character Teddy Tail, the Mouse. You had to create a design in the sand, working in some reference to Teddy Tail and, of course, the *Mail* and its popularity. Horace entered and employed Young Alf as his labourer, sending him running constantly to the rocks with a bucket to gather all the white stones he could find and quantities of different coloured seaweeds. While Alf laboured, Horace painstakingly built up his design showing a lighthouse, with Teddy Tail peering from a window and the beams of the light cunningly incorporating the *Daily Mail's* sales figure. He added a caption testifying to the newspaper's superiority above all others. At length, Alf having been graciously permitted to lay a few last pebbles and strips of black and green seaweed, the grand design was complete. A local photographer recorded it and the picture went off to Carmelite House. The Dellers' effort was declared the winning Margate entry and was rewarded by several of Lord Northcliffe's guineas.

Alfred was by this time attending Holy Trinity school, attached to the church which was to be destroyed in another war. He was a likeable little boy, neither exceptionally good nor noticeably bad. He was well built, more interested in games than in lessons, but with a serious, almost contemplative side to his nature, too. He seemed to be quite incapable of understanding mathematics; but his English, which he liked best, was good. The music taught at Holy Trinity was of merely rudimentary type, but at his next school, Salmestone Elementary, where he went at the age of nine, the music teacher, Mrs Hiscock, was something of an enthusiast, and certainly discerning, Alfred had not been at the school many weeks when, one music period, she gave his class *Cherry Ripe* to sing. After they had completed the first verse, Mrs Hiscock stopped them and told Alfred to sing the next verse as a solo.

'I sang it,' he recalled, 'and while I was doing so I

was suddenly conscious for the first time that my voice sounded somehow different from the other chaps'. And there also came an intense pleasure, a feeling of happiness and joy. The fact that I was singing alone like that, and feeling such sensations, did something for me personally in a very deep way. I couldn't have described any of it in words, but I was very conscious of it. In a sense, it was my beginning.'

TWO

Music at Salmestone School was taught by ear. The class songbooks contained only the words, the tunes being picked up from Mrs Hiscock's playing. Alfred learnt them all very quickly, while remaining in complete ignorance of the meaning of musical notation.

When he was eleven his name was entered as a candidate for a place at Margate Boys' Central School. This new and forward-looking establishment in fine surroundings, had been started after the war with a staff of ex-officers and progressive principles whose working out was already being watched with interest by many educational bodies. Competition for a place was keen, involving written and oral examinations. Alfred had worked hard at Salmestone and had hopes of succeeding, but for one obstacle: it was necessary to achieve a pass in mathematics. He sat the examination, and passed in everything—except mathematics.

Music and Mrs Hiscock came to the rescue. By one of those fortunate circumstances which punctuated Alfred Deller's life, the headmaster of Margate Boys' Central School chanced to be Mr W.H. Hiscock, his music teacher's husband. He called Alfred in for an interview, gave him to understand that it was only because his wife had pleaded with him to make an exception on account of the boy's musical promise, and agreed to admit him, on condition that he worked hard to get his maths up to the required standard. Much as he would have liked to repay the gesture, Alfred never succeeded. Mathematics and all scientific and technical subjects eluded his grasp throughout school life, and continued to do ever since.

He worked well at other subjects, especially English, and while he never distinguished himself in any classroom subject, he did not discredit himself. The school's system relied much upon the old wartime virtues of comradeship and fair play, and on co-operation between master and pupil. Merit marks were awarded for achievement, deducted for carelessness, laziness and unruliness, The worst penalty was to be known to one's house-fellows as the backslider who had let them down in the monthly merit shield competition. Alf Deller never let Gordon House down. Rather, he brought it credit in the sphere most certain to impress the greatest number of his fellows by being elected, in due course, captain of soccer and cricket and vice-captain of the school. A footballing team-mate remembered him as a 'gentle giant' of a right-back, hard and fearless in a tackle but using his strength only within the rules. When Alf Deller played cricket, everyone watched. As well as being the leading fast bowler he was a prodigious hitter, putting many a ball out of the ground and into the housing estate near by.

The other thing that was beginning to distinguish him from the mass of his fellows was his singing. Again, he was fortunate in an encounter. The music master at Margate Central was Roy Monkcom, a man of Polish extraction, still in his twenties and a dedicated teacher. He sensed at once that Alfred was not only a better singer than most, but that he possessed a deep latent interest in music and was eager to learn.

'He took a great interest in me,' Deller said. 'He took me to my first concerts. They were a revelation. We had no radio in those days and no proper orchestral music or serious song on our gramophone records. No one could pretend that Margate has ever been a musical centre, and those concerts were no great shakes; yet they held me riveted. Then, when I'd barely got over the first sensations, Monkcom taught me how to listen properly. Even at the first concert he started telling me how to dig with my ears, as it were, underneath the predominant tune and listen for the other things going on at the same time. What he was doing, I came to realise later, was to distinguish for me the musical form and the counterpoint. It may sound a simple and obvious thing to do, but its effect on a boy of twelve who knew nothing about music was nothing short of a revelation. I found I could do as he suggested very easily, so that from then onwards I ceased to look at the 'headlines' of a piece of music, but could absorb all the text together.

'I owe a great deal to Roy Monkcom. Shortly after I left the school he transferred to another outside Kent and I lost track of him, though I tried to get in touch. Many years later, when I had made something of a reputation, I was asked to sing in Handel's *Solomon* with the Reading Symphony Orchestra; and who should be leading the orchestra but Monkcom. It was a wonderful reunion.'

As well as learning something about music at school, Alfred was now singing regularly as a chorister at Margate Parish Church of St John the Baptist. Sergeant Deller had always insisted on regular attendance at church and Sunday School for all the children. Not all of them went gladly, but Alfred did. From his very first Sunday afternoon visit to a service at the Parish Church, when he was too young even to join the Sunday School, he had been sensitive to the atmosphere of church. St John the Baptist was a Low Church, with few mystical trappings to awe a small boy; but when his escorting sister showed him how to kneel, and he did so, with his nose only just reaching the ledge on which the hymnbooks lay, he smelt holiness, manifested in the cloth and glue of their bindings.

After doing his share of singing from the family pew for several years, Alfred put his name down for the choir, after the choirmaster, Hector Shallcross, had written to the Central School asking for recruits. He was eleven, and therefore a good two years above the ideal age for starting to be a chorister, but he was still singing treble, and Shallcross agreed to hear him. 'Very well, I'll take you,' he agreed afterwards, 'but you're really too old to make a singer.'

Except that he was a rather old treble, the new chorister made no noticeable impact on his fellows or on the music. Although both Mrs Hiscock and Roy Monkcom discerned in him a musical intelligence above the average, his promise seemed to extend little further. His singing was regarded with a certain respect by his school mates in tribute to an idol of the sportsfield. When he first appeared in a school concert, to sing the popular *Felix Keeps on Walking*, he had the audience thundering for more. Between that triumph and the next year's concert he had come under Monkcom's influence and developed more sober musical tastes, choosing for his second appearance the first Purcell air he was ever to sing to an audience, *I attempt from love's sickness to fly*. The entire school had greeted his arrival upon the stage with an ovation. When he gave them Purcell instead of Felix, he received what he termed 'the biggest raspberry of my career'.

At about this time he was promoted solo boy in the church choir. As such, he was invited to take part in a Sunday evening charity concert at the Margate Hippodrome, in a bill including conjurers, jugglers, and some comedy of a Sunday standard. Alfred wore his best suit, a plum colour, very fashionable at the time, which showed up spectacularly in the spotlight when he appeared for his solo number. The Sergeant and Mary from their seat in the balcony heard someone pass a facetious remark about it. The Sergeant leaned across and growled, 'You wait till you've heard him sing.' But Alfred's choice was again far removed from the popular ditties of the day. The audience returned him respect, rather than enthusiasm.

He spent four quite happy years at Margate Central School. He enjoyed music and English, and managed to bumble along successfully in everything not involving science or maths. His all-round sportsmanship kept him in continuous respect. So did his physique. He was big and sturdy, and could hold his own with any antagonist, though he did not choose to do so by returning physical violence. From an early age, school bullying had incensed him. While his size and strength excluded him from becoming a victim, he discovered a gift for rescuing weaker boys by talking the bullies out of their intentions, to the point of making them ashamed of themselves.

He was a keen Scout, living all the year round for the annual camp near Canterbury. The private parkland, the lake, the big house, the tent life, the camp fire, the walk to the little church at Bishopsbourne for Sunday morning service, all added up to the most romantic experience he had known. He was a fittingly romantic figure, with his big build, jet-black hair and swarthy, almost gipsy-like complexion. A contemporary paid him a striking tribute: 'One of the few people you can remember clearly when you look at a school photograph forty years later.'

He left school at fifteen. He had been luckier than his brothers and sisters, none of whom had enjoyed secondary education. Now, he had to fall into line. The Sergeant, who had known insecurity ever since leaving the army, had no doubt about what constituted a safe job for an unqualified youth or girl. Each of his children was eased into some branch or other of retail trade. Tom and Len had gone into furnishing, Em into millinery, Horace, after a year of odd jobs at 7s 6d a week, had broken the pattern slightly by entering an estate agent's. Alfred was earmarked for furniture, but it was another chance circumstance that decided just where he would begin his apprenticeship. A few weeks before leaving school he had played for the cricket eleven against a team from Munro Cobb, the Margate furnishers. In the first innings he took seven wickets for eight runs, and seven for twenty in the second. He was promptly offered a job, accepted it, and played for the firm's team for many years.

He faced his future philosophically. For a year or more he had been aware of inner stirrings. So far as he could rationalize them, they added up to a vague ambition to do something in music: he did not know what. All he did know was that the family's financial position, although now rather better with several members working, did not allow for passengers. 'I saw my life in terms of doing some job which would earn me a living, while music would remain a valued spare-time pleasure and consolation. When that job turned out to be selling furniture, I thought to myself, "Well, it might just as well be this as anything."'

He started at Munro Cobb in 1927 at seven and six-pence weekly, to be increased by half a crown every six months, Striped trousers and a dark jacket and waistcoat were *de rigueur* to the dignity of even a junior apprentice salesman. He would be required to spend a year in hard furnishings, one in soft, and so on through the departments, learning and selling as he progressed. He found serving at the counter embarrassing, becoming a nightmare whenever the moment came for calculating the prices of lengths of cretonne at 1s 11½d a yard. Attempts to use a ready reckoner merely added to his confusion. But he was not one to stay depressed for long. Behind-the-scenes larking with the other apprentices could be relied on to drive off any lingering gloom.

The gift of mimicry which helped to endear Alfred Deller to colleagues and friends throughout the world was evident even then. His best audience was female— Mr Munro Cobb's secretary and the cashiers. He was constantly in and out of their office with a new joke or impersonation. One afternoon, when Mr Cobb was out and no customers in sight, he noticed on a counter some Victorian fire-irons, beautifully polished, including a poker with an impressive knob on the end. A new Mayor of Margate had just been installed. Alfred dashed into the soft furnishing department to array himself in a colourful bedspread and a tea-cosy hat. Then, carrying the poker over his shoulder like a mace, he marched solemnly into the girls' office and reduced them to hysterics with a studied imitation of the Mayor making a speech of somewhat unmayoral character. Carried away by his eloquence, he did not pause to wonder why the girls' laughter had suddenly ceased. Mr Cobb, in the doorway behind him, cleared his throat. Fortunately, he was a boss who could share a joke.

There were several floors to the building, and a lift, beside each door of which was fitted a voice-pipe for inter-floor communication. You pulled out the plug and whistled to attract attention. Alfred achieved a perfect imitation of the wheezy whistle. The apprentices would wait until the old porter was polishing a floor at the far end of a department, then Alfred, hiding behind a piece of furniture, would whistle. Solemnly, the half-deaf man would put down his polisher and walk to the voice-pipe. His repeated 'allo?' was the confidently awaited pay-off.

One man at Munro Cobb for whom Alfred had nothing but deference was named Humphries. He was old, small, and wispy-haired, and resembled neither a sailor nor a poetry-lover. He was both. He had spent much of his life voyaging the world before the mast in sailing ships and his greatest love was poetry. He and Alfred got talking about it. The old man had written verse of his own, and it was this natural, primitive work which 'opened the great flood-gates' of poetic mood and mystery for the youth. Once more, Alfred Deller had had a fortunate encounter. Poetry was to matter more to him than he or his old sailor mentor ever came near to sensing.

He worked six days a week for the firm, spending most of his spare time out of doors. His footballing talent at school had been spotted and he had been given a trial for Margate Town Boys, which gained him a place in the team as full-back, leading in turn to selection for a trial game in the Kent Boys' team. In the summer months he played cricket for Margate. Off the sportsfield he was a Rover Scout and a member of the church youth organization, the King's Messengers.

Keeping up a connection with his school as a member

of a little band which attended the Old Boys' Association dances, Alfred played the drums, the first instrument he ever mastered. Becoming ambitious, he managed to buy a banjolele and learnt it easily. He was also slowly teaching himself to play the family piano.

A nightly custom, amusing or irritating to its regular witnesses, prevailed in the Deller household. At a certain hour the Sergeant would gravely draw out his watch, consult it for some moments, then say to Mary, 'Coming, mother?' Every night, Mary would answer, 'I don't know as I feel like going.' She and everyone else in the room knew what the Sergeant's reply would be: 'Well, we'd better get going, then.' Then they would rise, put on their outdoor clothes, and walk down to an old public house near by, the Sergeant for one glass of beer, Mary for a stout. They were not gossips who could make friends readily; the Sergeant's dignity and pride restrained him from reaching out to strangers. But they would chat a little to other customers of the pub, amongst them an old lady whose husband, it transpired, was an invalid who gave piano lessons for one shilling a time. The Sergeant offered to send Young Alf.

'I went about six or eight times. The old man was partially paralysed. He'd sit at the end of this terrible old walnut-cased piano, chain-smoking. I remember the great brown stains on his fingers, and the shaking hand holding the cigarette with the ash just managing to balance on the end. He tried to teach me *The Bluebells of Scotland* before some financial crisis brought the visits to an end. If you can call that tuition, it was all the tuition I ever had. I taught myself the rest, so, of course, my fingering is all over the place. My Bach playing, they tell me, is highly eccentric.'

His voice, in his mid-teens, was overdue to break, and there was no guarantee that he would find himself with a good adult one. Music of some sort seemed to be necessary to him, and his natural sense of pitch and interval, polished by regular choir work, gave good promise of success on some instrument or other. His teacher, Roy Monkcom, had suggested shortly before he left school that he try the violin. A dozen or more years after he had ceased to cry for 'the man with a stick on a piece of wood', Alfred began to save up the two pounds ten shillings needed for an old one Monkcom had found in a pawnshop. He asked his parents if, instead of giving him presents at Christmas and his birthday, they would put a little money aside for him. The shopkeeper agreed to reserve the fiddle, and in due course, and by many means, the money was raised, plus twelve and six for a bow. His sister Em, visiting Walworth Market in London one day with her husband, saw a music-stand for sale for half-a-crown. They bought it and carried it off to Margate for Alfred to use. He had started working by then, and could manage to find one and sixpence a time for lessons from a Mr Dyer.

He studied the violin for three years. He worked hard and picked it up naturally and quickly; but he soon found that violin-playing could never be more than a pastime. His fingers were long, except for the vital fourth finger of the left hand, which was disproportionately short. The G string was a difficulty for him from the beginning, and he could never manage it with facility. Still, he managed to become proficient enough to play the second part in the Bach Double Concerto. His mother made him a bag of green baize, tied round the neck with a black tape, for carrying the violin, until Tom found, in a junk shop, a battered old coffin-type case, bought and renovated it and presented it to his brother. Almost every member of the family, at one time or another, contributed somehow towards the gifted boy's progress. Deller always kept the violin, disintegrated but precious.

So, when he played at the Old Boys' dances, it was on the violin, with a repertoire ranging from the Palm Court kind of music to what was loosely called jazz. Another violinist, known as 'Squeaker' Evans, who heard him and was impressed, suggested that he might pick up some welcome cash by joining his trio, to play two nights a week in one of Margate's many small hotels during the summer season. Alfred did so and fulfilled a few engagements, not caring much for the music but glad to have the money. Glad, that is, to anticipate having the money, for when reckoning time came Squeaker was full of excuses but empty of cash. He proposed a settlement in kind. His father was a dealer in second-hand goods. If Alfred would care to go to the shop he could take his pick from several real leather, shaped violin cases. He did, and found himself professionally equipped at last.

He was not sorry that the job with the trio had folded up. Music, to him, was becoming something to be taken with increasing seriousness. He was very conscious of the dignity of the calling of musician, even if it was, in his case, only a spare-time adjunct to furniture selling. One evening he and Horace went to a local cinema in the High Street, where a film about the life of Liszt was being shown. The film was silent, the music for the appropriate piano passages being provided by the cinema pianist who strummed the usual accompaniment to the film. Alfred sat fascinated by his fellow musician's skill, and, when the film was over, marched down to the front, leaning over the brass rail and curtain which concealed the pianist from the audience to bestow warm praise, from one musician to another. When his brother asked him who he thought he was to make such pronouncements he replied that it had never occurred to him to wonder. The pianist had deserved praise: he had praised him.

The chief part of Alfred Deller's music-making, though, remained his work with the choir of St John the Baptist. He had quickly made a reputation as a soloist which had extended to various local concert platforms. At nearly sixteen he was still singing soprano. The choirmaster was baffled. In accordance with the belief that over-use of a boy's voice might be detrimental to his singing as a man, Mr Shallcross called

Alfred to him and told him he had better leave the choir.

The disappointment was tremendous, but the boy respected his choirmaster's knowledge of what was best for him. He sang for the last time at the parish Christmas party. One or two speeches were made in his praise. The vicar presented him with an inscribed silver watch. With a heart full of sadness at the thought that this might, for all he knew, mark the end of his days as a chorister, Alfred Deller made his way homeward.

THREE

If Margate was not exactly the hub of the musical universe, it was a thriving centre of entertainment of most other kinds. The charming little Georgian Theatre Royal had been closed since 1915 and would not re-open until 1930; but, in 1927, the Hippodrome flourished as the summer venue for all the top West End successes, with their original stars. During the winter, when audiences were harder to find, vaudeville and revue took over. Plays were presented at the Winter Gardens. Pierrots, concert parties and minstrels—the latter including the famous Uncle Bones and his troupe—flourished on the pier and elsewhere.

There was plenty of amateur entertainment, too. At the very moment that Alfred Deller was taking his sad farewell of the choir, another Margate resident, a Mr Crawshaw, charged with organizing evening entertainments in connection with a week's trade exhibition at the Winter Gardens, was looking for amateur acts to make up an all-male Nigger Minstrel bill. He had his tap-dancers, his cross-talk act, his interlocutor and enough minstrels to fill the stage nicely. All that remained was to select carefully the four voices for the quartet to sing the sentimental ballads essential to such a show. He had heard young Deller sing and thought his high voice would be ideal for the quartet's top line. He found Alfred willing, and within a few weeks the show was on, with a blacked-up Alfred Deller singing with the quartet in *Sweet and Law* and its like, and taking a solo spot with *Love's Old Sweet Song*, singing everything in the only way he knew how to sing, alto. Every night his solo got a tremendous hand. On the Saturday night, after the final show, he was removing his blacking in the dressing-room when Hector Shallcross appeared at his elbow, solemn-faced and shifting from one foot to the other.

'Well, Alfred, you're singing as well as ever. I don't understand it, but I can't lose you. *We* can't lose you. You'll have to come back to the choir and sing a bit of alto.'

So he returned to the choir stalls of the Church of St John the Baptist, no longer, now, standing in the front row with the boy sopranos, but behind and at the end; no longer singing the top line of the music, but the second, alto line. He knew nothing of the countertenor voice, its technique, historical background or tradition. He merely sang in his natural way, the same way, basically, as he would throughout his life. As he later explained:

'Many boys who sing, if they produce a bright, forward tone, are using a type of pharyngeal falsetto, with a head voice, not off their full vocal chords. In fact, the boys don't use that part of the voice for singing which they use for shouting. When they see someone across a field, and call, 'Hi, old so-and-so!', they produce a voice, as singers say, 'off the chest'. But when they sing they use this pharyngeal head quality.

'This is what I did then, and still do now. When I went back into the choir as an alto, instead of a soprano, there was no change at all in the way I used my voice. I merely sang the second line instead of the top. After a while, of course, I found that singing at a lower *tessitura* I had to use lower notes and not the upper fourth or fifth of my voice. It meant that I had to go down quite often to the ledger-lines below middle C, below G, and so on. This caused me some worry, because although I could produce those low notes, I couldn't give them any real resonance. The sound was inclined to disappear when I got round about the A or even B below middle C. I couldn't get any real bite.

'There was no one to whom I could turn to ask about it; and, if there had been, they wouldn't have known. So I simply had to evolve my own method of extending the resonance of my voice downward, and I now know that what I did by instinct and nature was the correct thing. This was to use all the forward sinus resonators and to take the voice, step by step, downward; moving from the head register I had used as a boy down into the chest register.

'This was really the point where my life as a counter-tenor began, as a boy of sixteen to seventeen singing simple alto parts in the church choir.'

Side by side with this instinctive change in his vocal technique there emerged suddenly a new awareness of music in the context of life, both in the personal and the broader sense. It made a deep and lasting impression on him.

'At that time the musical repertoire of the church depended very much on the Victorian composers. Not long after I returned to the choir Lent approached and Mr Shallcross started to prepare us for a series of mid-week services. One piece of music he chose as appropriate to the season was Orlando Gibbons' motet, *O Lord increase my Faith*.* Now, until this time I had known nothing of Tudor church music, let alone of Orlando Gibbons. One Friday evening we went through this motet for the first time, and I'm sure our first attempt was a pretty bad one. But as I sang my part it suddenly felt as though a door had been opened in Heaven. I had a sensation of immediate and complete fulfilment; and as we reached that marvellous combination of the music and the words in the last page I knew certainly that from that moment the music of this period would be my life.

'It would be many more years before I would sing such music at all frequently. But I think that experience placed me in the true centre of my life. I have believed since then that life can only make sense within a spiritual context; that everything is related to the

---

*Now known to have been composed by Henry Loosemore (? 1600–1670). It was sung at Alfred Deller's funeral by the Deller Consort.

spiritual, and that the arts are an extension of man's spiritual nature. This was the first inkling I had of it, and it was a most incredible feeling.'

Another experience, outside the church this time, added to this sense of revelation.

'It happened one November night. I had just left a choir practice at which we had been preparing carols for Christmas from a new volume called the *New English Carol Book*. It was a night of bright moonlight, and frost was gleaming on the road and the fences and gates of the houses as I walked through the unromantic council-housing estate at Margate, where we had moved into one of the first houses to be completed. As my footsteps rang in the stillness there was going through my head the tune of one particular carol:

> As up the wood I took my way
> The night began to fall,
> And all around the snow lay white
> And I heard a sweet voice call.

'Suddenly—and I could point out even now the very spot where this happened—I was overwhelmed by a feeling of joy and complete happiness of indescribable intensity. I felt that whatever might happen to me in life would be for the best; that something had, as it were, taken me over completely and was going to organize my life to be everything that I wished it to be. It was an amazing feeling of exaltation, shot through with a pure joy that I have only felt once since, and that many years later. Often, in times of stress and anxiety, I have recalled that experience and been comforted immediately.'

The feeling for poetry, kindled and fanned by old Mr Humphries, was intensifying, too. Another boy, Fred Crispe, also a violinist, with whom he playet duets, shared his fondness for such things. They would take long walks together on winter's nights, along the Cliftonville cliffs to Kingsgate, with the wind driving them forward and the sea spray sheeting up over the cliff edge. It was as near to romantic intensity as one could aspire at Margate, and he would return home in the grip of it all and write verses of his own:

A Jay and a Magpie adazzle the winter sun
And shake the stark fingers of the lichened tree
Dancing a pattern on the heavy earth.
A shaft of swift perception pierces the Time-Locked door
And I am oned in the perfect dance of the eternal now.

On a less exalted level he went on playing his fiddle at the Old Boys' hops, and, eager for every kind of musical experience, took up someone's suggestion that he might join the Margate Amateur Opera Group. Arriving at the hotel where rehearsals for an operetta, or some such work, were in progress, he was interviewed by a harassed musical director.

'What do you sing?'

'Alto.'

'Alto! Oh, well, get over there amongst the girls.'

He never attended again.

In 1929 a blow fell which knocked mere musical preoccupations into second place: he got the sack. The depression had set in. Kindly old Mr Munro Cobb, hating the circumstances which had forced him to do it, called Alfred in one day and explained as gently as he could that economies had to be made and the junior staff with no wives or children to support must be the first to go.

Much as he hated joining the Labour Exchange queue to draw the dole, Alfred soon had cause to be thankful for the few shillings it brought in each week. Four months passed by with no other job in sight and the deepening depression making it less and less likely that one would ever come his way. Then, in the seventeenth week, yet another of those seemingly chance circumstances which directed his life came to his rescue and set another course for his destiny.

A member of the St John the Baptist church congregation had invited a friend from St Leonard's-on-
Sea, adjoining Hastings, Sussex, to spend a weekend
at Margate, and took him along to a church social
function at which Alfred sang several solos. The visitor,
who happened to be sub-organist of Christ Church, St
Leonard's, was much impressed. He approached the
young soloist afterwards to ask if he would object to
his mentioning him to his organist, Dr Allan Biggs, a
member of the well-known musical family. Christ
Church, he added, was a wealthy and influential church,
and there was a good chance that if Alfred were accepted
for the choir a job could also be found for him. The
offer was gladly accepted.

In due course a letter arrived, inviting him to spend
a weekend at Hastings, and a few days later he found
himself a guest in the house of a Miss Jakeham, a pillar
of Christ Church. It was a household in the Dickensian
style, lit by open gas jets without mantles. Miss Jakeham, a semi-invalid of great gentility, lay on her couch
all day attended by a manservant with a vast handlebar
moustache and an unchanging expression of deep
gloom, who brought her constant relays of hot-water
bottles. She loved talking to young men and was soon
assuring Alfred of her influential support. Christ Church
was, and still is, an advanced Anglo-Catholic church.
High Mass that Sunday was a new experience for Alfred,
the liturgy and atmosphere fascinating him immediately.
After the service he went up into the organ gallery to
sing, to Allan Biggs's accompaniment, for the rector,
Father Roberts. By the time he had finished Father
Roberts's face was radiant. 'We *must* have you,' he
declared. 'We will do all we possibly can to get you
here.'

Alfred returned to Margate and the dole. Every day
he waited eagerly for the postman, and every day there
was nothing from St Leonard's. Then, one afternoon
while he was pottering in the garden shed, knocking
together some props for an amateur dramatics produc-

tion, his mother came down the path, apprehensively fingering the buff envelope of that rare form of communication with the Deller household, a telegram. Trembling almost as much as she, Alfred ripped it open. It read, 'COME TO CANTERBURY NEXT WEEK FOR INTERVIEW FOR POSSIBLE JOB IN HASTINGS.'

Why he should have been summoned to Canterbury was explained when he found himself being interviewed at Lefevre's department store by the chairman-director of the Drapery Trust, another of whose businesses was the large general furnishing house of Plummer Roddis at Hastings. Alfred was offered a salesman's job with this firm, to start in a few weeks' time. He accepted. Looking for a temporary job for him in the meantime, Allan Biggs approached the much smaller firm of Elijah Gray & Sons, Ltd, Complete House Furnishers and Undertakers, 138, London Road, St Leonard's-on-Sea. On that very day, as it happened, the firm's salesman had gone down with scarlet fever: the offer of a temporary hand was accepted with alacrity. Once more, unbeknown to him, Fate had set Alfred Deller upon one of the major paths of his life.

He went to live in Hastings feeling himself to be a marked man. Life's obliging way of opening a door whenever another had closed behind him had not escaped his notice. He had no doubt at all who was responsible. God had shown Himself unto Young Alf Deller. He was humbly grateful, awed, yet determined not to play the hypocrite about it. If God had picked him out to be one of His musicians, then a Musician he was going to be seen to be. Disregarding the fact that God had arranged primarily for him to sell furniture at thirty-five shillings a week plus commission on sales, with part-time singing in addition for another twenty-six pounds a year, he hastened off to a chain store to select a black, double-breasted coat, reaching almost to his ankles, a black, broad-rimmed hat of the style reputedly favoured by assassins and anarchists, and a black-and-white silk polka-dot choker. Thus arrayed, he arrived in Hastings, and the populace wondered.

He found good lodgings, with full board and part of his laundry included, for twenty-five shillings a week, which left a gratifying weekly balance. A little later he moved to share rooms with two young and jolly veterinary assistants, lodging next door to the shop. They made a high-spirited trio and one of the others, Rodney Pickett, remained a life-long friend. A few weeks after arriving, Alfred had moved over to Plummer Roddis as arranged. He found he was required to live in with the other salesmen, and hated it. 'It was like something out of *Kipps*,' he recalled.* After a week he returned to Elijah Gray's, and his destiny.

Elijah Gray had founded the family firm in the previous century. On his death it had passed to his seven sons and one daughter. Possessing more commercial acumen than any combination of her brothers, the daughter had bought them out one by one and now exercised sole control over the flourishing little firm. She had parted from a charming, artistic, but unreliable husband, named Lowe, when her only child, Peggy, was a few years old. For nearly ten years since she had devoted herself to her business and her daughter, and maintained a completely platonic companionship with an old friend, a kindly married man whose wife was permanently confined in an institution.

Peggy, at the time of Alfred's arrival, was about his own age, a trim, vivacious little blonde, working as secretary to the editor of the local newspaper, the *Hastings Observer*. She was as startled as everyone else by the new arrival's mode of dress, but quickly recognized that the affectation sprang from ingenuousness, not conceit, and that there was more to him than met the eye. Her mother saw it, too, and it worried her. She

---

*Readers familiar with H.G. Wells's *Kipps* may have noticed other similarities between young Kipps and young Deller. An added coincidence is that it was by Plummer Roddis (Folkestone branch) that Kipps was employed.

found his charm immense, his high spirits and ready flow of good talk instantly disarming, his manly build and dark good looks fascinating. Having herself fallen for a charmer, to her cost, she was determined that her daughter should make no such mistake. Before long, she was taking every care to keep her attractive young salesman well in his place. It was made clear that he would be 'Deller', the junior shop-hand, and nothing more. And, as she admitted to him years later, a stronger reason for her restraint towards him developed with time, as instinct told her that Deller would sooner or later have to choose between the security of settled employment and the hazards of professional life. There were plenty of music-lovers amongst her customers ready to tell Mrs Lowe that her employee's talents were of no common order.

Hastings was one of the leading musical centres of the provinces. The resident Municipal Orchestra, under its permanent conductor Julius Harrison, gave symphony concerts every Friday evening, Sunday afternoon and Sunday evening, with a 'pop' on Saturday evening. World-famous artists appeared with it, and in course of time, and for an expenditure of sixpence a seat, Alfred heard playing of a kind he had never known by such soloists as Casals, Rachmaninov and other artists of fame.

Christ Church possessed a magnificent Willis organ, and, in Dr Allan Biggs, one of the best organists in the country. Easter Day, when the strings and timpani of the Municipal Orchestra would join the choir in the west gallery for a Haydn or Mozart Mass, always produced an indelible memory for Deller. Equally, Biggs was an authority on plainsong, having helped to edit the first English manual. All the great chants for Holy Days were performed at Christ Church, with, to Deller, unforgettable effect and more than a touch of influence upon his own singing.

'I found I had a natural affinity with plainsong. I have never ceased to feel that the singing of Gregorian chant should be part of the basic training of all singers. You are not bound to a bar line. You are free to float along on those great, long flowing phrases. I think that, imperceptibly, the singing of plain-chant early in my career affected my approach to phrasing, quite apart from the other effects this finest form of church music had on me.'

The beauty of its liturgy, for which Christ Church was renowned, and the new-found attraction of the Catholic form of worship there, overwhelmed Alfred's romantic soul. He was tempted instinctively to commit himself all the way by joining the Roman Catholic church. After examining the prospect keenly and thinking deeply, however, he found himself unable to accept the tenet of absolute papal authority, so let the idea drop. The Anglo-Catholic attitude, both in its degree and its historical background, he found entirely satisfactory. One of the first of a succession of clergymen who had a cumulative influence on Alfred Deller's life was a priest at Christ Church at the time, the late Lance Mellor, founder of the Christ Church Homes for home- less children. He had a wonderful sense of humour, always organizing the Christmas pantomime and taking the Dame's part. Speaking of him, Deller used an expression often echoed in other people's references to himself: 'He really lived his Christianity out to the full; not only in church, but carrying it through into his whole life.'

Father Mellor's magnetic personality quickly drew Alfred into many of his youth activities. He became a keen member of the Christ Church Younger Com- munity. They met in friends' houses to listen to lectures, discuss and read plays. This led to the formation of the Christ Church Dramatic Society, with Alfred Deller, of the persuasive tongue and commanding confidence, as producer. One of their first productions was *The Eternal Spring*, a three-act situation comedy about an archaeologist who marries his secretary for the sake of convenience, and falls in love with her later. The part

of Nockles, 'a suave and efficient butler', was played
by the producer, his first appearance on the dramatic
stage; and the leading role of Mary, the 'charming yet
unsophisticated' secretary, was acted impressively by
Peggy Lowe.

Despite her mother's determination to keep her well
away from the young salesman, amateur dramatics and
religion began to bring her daughter into frequent
contact with the dangerous charmer. Although she had
done no acting before, Peggy had accepted with enthusiasm his suggestion that she join the Christ Church
Players. Her lively personality had quickly made its
mark on the company and its audiences, so that she
generally found herself in a leading rôle. She had not
been a regular churchgoer previously, but now began
to attend every week and took Confirmation. Circumstances had also decreed that she and Alfred should see
a good deal of one another during their daily work,
for Peggy had by now left her job at the newspaper to
act as her mother's secretary.

Mrs Lowe took firm steps to counteract any possible
effects of this increased proximity. In Deller's first
months with the firm he had been treated to outings
in the family car, with Mrs Lowe driving and Peggy
as his fellow passenger, tea at some point on the journey,
and a pleasant, polite chatter all the way. Now, these
jaunts ceased. Deller's morning greetings to his employer were returned coldly, if at all, and conversation
confined strictly to business. Mrs Lowe's discouraging
tactics were at first less necessary than she supposed.
Peggy liked Alfred well enough, but was by no means
smitten. She was attractive, popular, the daughter of a
well-to-do, respected family, and consequently did not
lack other admirers whose background and means
contrasted markedly with those of a young shopman.
At one stage her mother deliberately set out to encourage other young men, some of them with cars of
their own, to squire Peggy about, giving her unlimited
time off from her desk for the purpose. Often, Alfred

watched from behind the counter as Peggy ran out with her swimming things, to be driven off in a sports car.

The feeling this provoked was not quite one of pain; he had not set his cap at Peggy. Yet, deep down, each recognised a mutual attraction and found it intensifying. Alfred had always got on well with the other sex. He had had plenty of girl friends; but this time he felt differently. For her part, Peggy tried to rationalize herself out of whatever it was she seemed to be feeling for him, only to come up against the notion that there was an indefinable something more to him than to any of the other young men. He bought her flowers and wrote poems to her—even if he did use the backs of linoleum tiles for the purpose. Without going so far as to declare their feelings for one another, the young couple tacitly acknowledged them. To placate Mrs Lowe they agreed to spend less time together outside working hours, and see what effect it produced.

The effect on Alfred surprised him. Admitting to himself what he had never before allowed himself to believe, that he had been on the brink of love and marriage, he thought he recognized another of God's emphatic signals, Yes, there it was, perfectly clear: God had earmarked Alfred Deller for a priest. He went for counsel to the priests at Christ Church. They were at once pleased and encouraging. He was serious-minded, fervently identified with the church in both its spiritual and social rôles, and the possessor of mature gifts of understanding and compassion. They assured him of their support for his candidature; but, suddenly, instinct made him draw back. He had been mistaking emotional reaction for true vocation. Still, he wavered for several months before asking Peggy to go about with him again. She was as relieved as he; they acknowledged their love.

One evening, when he had seen Peggy back to the foot of her stairs, the landing light snapped on and Mrs Lowe appeared, grim-faced.

'Go to bed, Peggy,' she ordered. 'I want to speak with Deller.'

He went up apprehensively and took a seat in the drawing-room. At once, to his deep embarrassment, his employer began to cry, pouring out recriminations on him for wishing to take an only daughter away from a lonely woman. He, reasonably, replied that she was depriving a lonely man of a wife. Then the tears ceased, but as she saw him to the door Mrs Lowe added, 'I can't depend that you aren't going to run off at the first opportunity to go on with this mad singing business.' Alfred returned to his lodgings feeling too bewildered to know whether to be happy or dejected.

Eventually Mrs Lowe resignedly accepted defeat. Although her future son-in-law remained plain 'Deller' in the hearing of customers, in private the surname was dropped, though not in favour of his christian name: intimacy was signified by his being addressed as nothing at all. Materially, the signs were much more encouraging. Having capitulated, Mrs Lowe suddenly found she could not do enough to help. Alfred's salary was increased. He was regarded as shop manager. An uncle of Peggy's, a master builder, began construction of a nice house for them in a pleasant part of St Leonard's.

In the quietness of his room, Alfred took stock of his situation. The prospect was far from alarming. He had never known security. He had no capital and had never earned much more than his living and modest pleasures demanded. He was about to step up to a respected level of the community, with a house, a good salary with a position of authority, and, not least, a wife whom he loved deeply. The business of Elijah Gray & Sons Ltd. was well-established, with the satisfactory turnover for those days of some £9,000 a year, and Mrs Lowe had made it quite clear that it would eventually be left to Peggy and himself. Meanwhile, she was insisting upon giving them all they needed in the way of furnishings and other household necessaries.

The thought that he might be selling such things to

other people for the rest of his days did not daunt him. Only the lesser part of him seemed to be involved in the business, whose demands he met automatically. It also brought him into pleasant contact with all sorts of people. He was frequently out of the shop, visiting people's homes to estimate for carpets and curtains, and advise on furnishings. Often, an absence would extend hours longer than the needs of duty. Mrs Lowe fretted and fumed, 'Where has that man got to?', knowing full well that he and his customers would be engrossed in some conversation on any topic under the sun except their furnishing problems. So, his working life was tolerable, even pleasant. As to music, things were moving encouragingly enough. Dr Biggs was a friend of Mrs Lowe, who willingly met his requests that Alfred should have time off on all saints' days to sing in the church. When Biggs went to some other parish to give a special recital or inaugurate a new organ he usually took Alfred with him as special soloist. The Press had begun to notice him: 'Mr Alfred Deller (a remarkable male alto)'; 'Mr Deller, the eminent alto.' 'A most impressive feature of the evening was the surprising quality and perfect control of Mr Alfred Deller's alto voice, which has unlimited power combined with the greatest delicacy. His rendering of "O Thou that tellest" and "He shall feed his flock" was an experience not to be forgotten by the large congregation.'

Not all his notices had been quite impartial. Allan Biggs happened also to be the music critic for the *Hastings Observer* and a local correspondent for the *Morning Post* (now the *Daily Telegraph*). Still, it was gratifying to a beginner to read any sort of praise, and when he sang in places other than church, where applause was in order, his audiences left him in no doubt of the sincerity of what Biggs had written. His biggest chance yet had come in an invitation to sing at one of the Municipal Orchestra's concerts. He performed two groups of English songs with piano. 'The sensation of this concert,' ran the newspaper report, 'was the appearance of Alfred Deller, the possessor of an alto voice of almost incredible beauty. He astonished the enthusiastic audience in two groups of Old English songs by the total absence of effort with which he used his voice, which is capable of infinite light and shade from a full, rich tone down to a mere whisper. It is a long time since we heard anything as touching as his singing of "Willow, Willow", "Drink to me only", and the other examples of fine English songs which he gave. Mr Deller's intonation and articulation are as perfect as the way he produces those silvery tones, unusual enough in a lady, but in a man, phenomenal.'

Even if Allan Biggs had written it, it was no more than the truth. Deller appeared many more times at the White Rock Pavilion, and sang in many more churches. In an article on 'Hastings as music centre' in the *Morning Post*, Richard Capell, paying tribute to the distinction of Christ Church choir's work under Allan Biggs, concluded, 'The Christ Church Choir possesses an alto soloist whose match one could go far without finding.'

Years earlier, Young Alf Deller had confided to a sister-in-law his burning desire to set foot on the ladder of musical progress. A decade had passed since then. His technique and understanding of music had developed side by side. He had made a small name in a limited district. As he sprawled in his room now, taking stock of his life on the eve of marriage, he knew that the odds in favour of his becoming widely renowned were slight. He was twenty-five. Many celebrated soloists had been noticed well before that age. Apart from the guidance of choirmasters he had had no musical training, had attended no conservatoire: what he knew he had found out for himself. His voice, moreover, was of the rarest and least useful kind. The male alto voice, as generally known, was a curiosity of limited ability, little art, and associated with that unpleasant hooting sound, heard only fleetingly above the more manly voices, which had gained it the label of 'owl-to'. There could be little prospect of solo work for such a voice; and what there was would be in a class of music that would appeal only to an esoteric minority.

Yet, though these were familiar thoughts to Alfred Deller, they had never managed to depress him. When he sang Sterndale-Bennett's *O Lord, Thou hast searched me out*, he expressed his own conviction. Some weeks later, visiting the half-built house with Peggy, he was seized with sudden panic. Were they building him a prison? He blurted out, 'Peggy, I hope you'll understand this: although there's no sign of anything at present, you must know that if my chance to get on as singer ever does come up I may feel I have to go after it without thought for anything else.'

Peggy replied, 'Don't worry. We'll live it as it comes.'

They were married on 5 June, 1937.

FOUR

The wedding took place, of course, at Christ Church, conducted by Father Frank Steel. There was a full nupital mass, Palestrina's *Aeterna Christi Munera*, and the whole occasion, on a scorching day, seemed as magnificent as a coronation through which Peggy passed, friends reported later, with a fixed smile and a glazed stare. They went off to honeymoon near Honiton, Devon, at a pleasant little hotel on the River Otter, from which guests were invited to catch their own trout for breakfast. After a blissful week they returned to St Leonard's, where their house was ready for them to move in, and Alfred squared himself to face his future as a businessman.*

It was at this time that he began to be deeply concerned about social questions. The Christian observances which gave him such deep spiritual and romantic satisfaction had somehow ceased to be enough.

'I felt that if Christianity really meant anything at all it should be lived out in practical terms of sociological work. If we believed that Christ is the Incarnate Son of God, then the logical implication of the Incarnation was that all of life, everything in life, is sanctified through Christ. The heart of all degrees of Catholicism is the blessed sacrament. I had gradually come to see that the presence of our Lord in the sacrament means that the whole of life *is* sacrament: that everything in our relationships with one another, in our politics and

---

*An additional argument with which Mrs Lowe had tried to dissuade Peggy from marrying him was to be reffected throughout his career in a mistaken belief about the physical make-up of a singer with so high a voice. 'He's not a complete man, you know,' she had warned her daughter. It is enough to relate that a few months after their marriage Peggy began her first pregnancy. There are two sons and a daughter.

in our social work, is sanctified. I felt this very strongly. Some of my views were called "Bolshie" by certain people who believed the church should keep out of everything except its spiritual functions. In a sense, I suppose they were right. My attitude in those days may have been a sort of Christian communism; it was certainly nothing to do with political Communism.'

He became an active worker for his beliefs, encouraged by his rector and enthusiastically supported by Peggy and their fellow members of the Christ Church Young Group. The church was situated in a poor district of mean back streets, in which many old people lived in wretched conditions. The young men and women of Christ Church went round to clean up for them and, with paint and wallpaper, tried to repair the dilapidations of age and neglect. It was their practical gesture. Otherwise, their activities consisted mainly of discussions amongst themselves. Regular Sunday evening meetings were held, with guest speakers invited by Alfred. A Fascist spoke to them one week, a Communist the next. The members discussed both points of view and then, on the third Sunday, the speakers were invited to come back and join them in listening to the Christian sociological point of view, expressed by Father W.G. Peck, at that time principal of the Industrial Christian Fellowship.

They also discussed pacifism. Alfred's feelings about it had long roots. His childhood had been passed under the stern rule of a man for whom militarism was the supreme creed. Sergeant Deller's notion of conducting a good conversation was to repeat for the umpteenth time the familiar yarns of his experiences in India and South Africa. 'Boast, boast, boast!' a daughter-in-law remembers Mary whispering as they passed in the doorway with tea things while the Sergeant held forth in the parlour. That same daughter-in-law, Mrs Beatrice Deller, described the whole family, the Sergeant excepted, as people incapable of hurting even a beetle.

Alfred Deller also recalled the effect on him as a boy

of his parents' overheard quarrels. He would lie in bed terrified by their shouting, fearful that the next thing he would hear would be blows. It made all violence a distasteful, degrading thing. At the cinema he had seen *All Quiet on the Western Front, Hell's Angels* and *Journey's End*. Their picture of the carnage and wastage of war appalled him, and many of their scenes stayed vividly in his mind all his life. One of his best friends at Margate Central was a boy named Harry Kinlan, a member of Alfred's house and a fellow-member of the football team.* They spent much time together during the summer holidays, bathing, swimming, lying on the sands, or playing about with a tennis ball. One day they were kicking the ball against the wall of Westbrook Pavilion, pausing from time to time to sit and talk. During one of these interludes Alfred suddenly remarked, 'You know, it's absolutely fantastic, this business of soldiers going out to fight face-to-face. I bet before long there'll be just one man on each side with his finger on a button. All they'll need to do is press the buttons and each other's cities will just be disintegrated.' Startled by this vision, the boys went back to kicking their ball. But the appalling notion never left at least one of them.

The Christ Church Dramatic Society 'enhanced an already good reputation' by presenting J.B. Priestley's *Laburnum Grove*, produced by Alfred Deller, who also played the parts of Bernard Baxley and Sergeant Morris. The local newspaper critic described him in the former rôle as 'mirth-maker in chief'. He went on, 'Looking remarkably like a caricature of Hitler, with a long black lock of hair over his forehead and a small moustache—and wearing loud check plus fours—Alfred Deller was a fit subject for laughter before he had opened his mouth, and some of his lethargic observations were extremely funny.'

Peggy also came in for praise, prophetically enough,

---

*To be awarded the George Medal as a fireman in the London blitz.

as Mrs Radfern, 'whose faith in her husband nothing could shake'.

It was their last stage appearance together. Shortly after, Peggy withdrew from the more arduous social engagements; and on 27 September 1938, just before Neville Chamberlain returned from Munich triumphantly waving his scrap of paper, the Dellers' first child, Mark, was born. In hospital, Peggy had been refused newspapers during the crisis days. Now, with 'peace in our time' seemingly assured, the future promised unending bliss. Before long, however, a mutual restlessness began to affect the new parents. Peggy recalls, 'I suddenly had the awful feeling that "this was it". Alfred and I seemed to have got all we could expect to have in life, and there was nowhere further for us to go, nothing to aim for. Alfred felt the same. We discussed it, and felt ashamed of ourselves for having almost too much. The thought that his music might be the key to our future never occurred to me, though I think it was constantly in his mind that he would become a professional musician. To me, his music was just his hobby. I had almost ceased to think about it.'

Their gloomy thoughts soon passed under the pressure of new events. With Mark's first birthday less than a month away, war broke out.

As a married man, aged twenty-seven, with a child, Alfred did not immediately qualify for conscription. His work at the shop and his singing at Christ Church continued uninterrupted. For some time the war touched him only lightly. Peggy's mother, sharing a widely held fear that gas attacks were imminent, had gas-proofed one of the large basement rooms of her combined home and business premises. Peggy was pressed to bring Mark to shelter there whenever a siren sounded, and before long Alfred was agreeing to close up their new home and move with the family into permanent quarters in Mrs Lowe's substantial three-storied building.

They had not been there long when he came home

from Evensong one day with a copy of the *Church Times*. Ensuring that they were out of her mother's earshot, he explained to Peggy that a bass singer, Percy Sutton, better known to his fellow choristers as 'Laddie', had pointed out to him an advertisement of vacancies for a bass and alto in Canterbury Cathedral choir. Assuring each other that they had little chance of succeeding, they agreed to have a try, subject to family consent. All the way home Alfred had been thinking not so much of the stiff audition he could expect to face as the explosion his proposal would touch off in Mrs Lowe's household. Even Peggy might be expected to object. If he were, by some long chance, appointed to Canterbury, it would mean the disruption of their domestic arrangements, and a new threat to their financial security. The pay would be small and it would be necessary for him to find a part-time job, so he would not have much time to devote to his family. Worst of all loomed the possibility of a row between Peggy and her mother which might have permanent consequences.

To his relief, Peggy raised no objections. If this was what he wanted, then it was what she wanted. The upheaval could be borne somehow. They went to her mother and told her together. Her reaction was surprisingly mild. Without quite saying, 'I told you so!', she merely assured them the whole idea was mad, with no possible future for them. This unexpectedly reasonable opposition caused Alfred a moment of second thought. It was Peggy who determined him. Looking beyond all practical considerations, she saw that it was a thing he must try, or for ever regret. The application went in.

It was not his first shot at a cathedral post. In 1930 he had applied for an alto vacancy at Lincoln, backed by warm commendations from his then present and former vicars at Margate. In spite of the latter's assertion that 'the choir would be fortunate which secured his services', Lincoln declined them. Three years later he had tried for the vacant alto lay clerkship at Salisbury Cathedral, with Hector Shallcross's testimonial to his undoubted gifts. Once again he was disappointed.

Canterbury, with one of the country's oldest choral traditions, promised to be no easier. Without holding any inflated opinion of his talents, he knew that his voice, with its unusual range over nearly two octaves from G below middle C to G flat, was well capable of all demands it might meet, in solo or in concert. His musicianship had never been criticized. He had full confidence in his ear and instinctive intonation. His choral experience now totalled seventeen unbroken years, more than half of which had been spent in the notable Christ Church choir under the first-rate supervision of Allan Biggs. And—a thing he knew was by no means the case with all professional cathedral choristers—he was a devout Christian and churchman, with an intense feeling for, and understanding of, the spiritual function of church music.

Against these assets, he was conscious of one deficiency which, in the eyes of a Cathedral Establishment, might nullify them all: he had no formal qualifications. Cathedral appointments tend to be made on a 'closed shop' basis. He had belonged to no Cathedral school, attended no academy; had, in fact, had no tuition at all. Everything he knew he had found out for himself, and everything he could do he had learned as his own teacher. That could condemn him, for a start. His dedicated seriousness of intention was as apparent to himself as to those who had worked with him, but it might not appear so readily at a single interview. His capacity for self-discipline was immense: he could not otherwise have achieved what he had; yet a long dependence on self-discipline, he knew, sometimes made the demands of teamwork hard to accept. Many self-made men, in more spheres than music, had been rejected instinctively by those who saw any individualist as a potential underminer of meek conformity.

Perhaps the reason why his decision to try for the

Canterbury post, with all it would bring in terms of upheaval and dissent, had not caused more rumpus was because it was outside the belief of Mrs Lowe, or Peggy, or even himself, that anything would come of it. But if it should, he told himself, it would represent the fulfilment of a dream he had cherished quietly since his earliest days in the choir of St John the Baptist, Margate. In those days regular Choral Union festivals were still held in Canterbury Cathedral, at which massed choirs from all over Kent took part in a spectacular service. He had gone with the St John's choir, and been overwhelmed by it all: the glory, the shared experience, the massed music in the ancient place of pilgrimage and martyrdom. Later, when he was a little older, he had taken a bus from Margate to Canterbury in order to attend Evensong. He had sat alone this time, listening to the cathedral choir sing the Mendelssohn anthem *Lo, everyone that thirsteth, come to the fountain*. It had been one of the deepest experiences of his young lifetime. The idea of ever being able to attend the cathedral every day, and occupy one of the choir stalls and sing, had remained his vision of utter bliss.

With such conflicting fears and hopes writhing in his mind, and dressed in his best dark suit, with his gas mask in its little cardboard box looking more absurd than ever slung from his shoulder, Alfred took the train to London to answer a summons to an interview by Dr Gerald Knight, then organist at Canterbury Cathedral, later Director of the Royal School of Church Music. Dr Knight heard him sing and told him that his name would be on the short list. The Precentor, Canon Joseph Poole, later Precentor of Coventry Cathedral, asked him to read a passage from the sermons of John Donne, his customary yardstick for judging anyone's understanding of English. 'Laddie' Sutton had reached the short list, too, and a few days later they travelled together to Canterbury to sing in the cathedral itself, before the Dean and Chapter. Sutton, who had started it all, was told that he had not been appointed.

Alfred Deller carried back to St Leonard's the news that he had been offered the post of alto lay clerk.

He was expected to take up the appointment immediately. The chief problem it posed was accommodation. With the disruptions of war, and evacuation, there was little hope of finding a family home in Canterbury. It was agreed that, for the time being at any rate, Peggy and Mark should stay with her mother and Alfred should accept an offer of a room in the home of his brother Horace, who was working for a tailor in Canterbury and living there with his wife.

The next difficulty was one of economics. A lay clerk's pay was three pounds a week. It was the accepted thing that the men could take other work, but their cathedral duties left them with few consecutive hours a week in which to give an employer his money's worth. Alfred managed to find work with Court's, the furnishing firm, for thirty shillings a week. If Peggy were to join him, they would have under five pounds a week for all their needs. While she remained with her mother she was well provided for and comfortable and wanted for nothing—except her husband. He began to look for a place to rent in Canterbury.

It was the period of the 'phoney war', before the fall of France, and life in Canterbury still moved along more or less normally. All the cathedral services continued to be held, with their usual large congregations. Deller had leisure to savour the supreme delight, as he found it, of singing the finest examples of English church music in one of her greatest cathedrals, although one of his first appearances in his choir stall coincided with an unspiritual contretemps sufficient to disillusion any novice.

The Dean at the time was the late Dr Hewlett Johnson, the celebrated 'Red Dean' of Canterbury, between whom and other senior clergy feelings were, as so often, running high. A leader of the opposition was the late Canon J.M.C. Crum, self-styled as 'God's Protestant' with the function of protecting all that he considered to be in the name of God, Christianity and English churchmanship against the 'Red Dean'. It was Canon Crum's turn of duty as Vice-Dean on the afternoon of Deller's first Evensong.

'It was two minutes to three, and we stood waiting in that wonderful old Treasury Chapel, with the sun streaming through the windows and everything quiet except for the ticking of the clock. I was almost overwhelmed by the atmosphere of calm and beauty. Then, at a minute to three, the Dean came sailing in, not yet vested, passed between the aisles of the boys and men with a cheerful, "Umm, good afternoon gentlemen, good afternoon boys," and vanished into the Treasury. I noticed that Canon Crum, standing next to me, turned his back on him as he passed. As the clock struck three the Dean called out from the Sacristy, in the friendliest of voices, "Umm, will you carry on, please, Mr Vice-Dean?" There was a moment's pause before Canon Crum shrieked back, "No, I won't!" I stood there petrified, waiting to see what would happen next, conscious of the old Canon next to me white and drawn, absolutely furious. Then, after another minute or two, out sails the Dean, as though nothing in the world has happened, and, "Umm, let us pray." It was an incredible initiation for me into cathedral life.' *

Soon after his brother's arrival in Canterbury, Horace Deller left his employment and went away to work in Bognor Regis with the National Assistance Board, while waiting to be called up into the Royal Air Force. Alfred managed to find lodgings, to which he could at last bring Peggy and Mark, in the house of a woman whose husband was away with the Forces. She had two children and did not care to be left alone. After

---

*An even more startling initiation would have been at that Evensong at another, nameless, cathedral, which provided one of his most-repeated ecclesiastical anecdotes. A lay clerk who had imbibed unwisely in the earlier part of the afternoon was about to sing a solo. The organ had just finished the introduction when the man changed his mind, turning instead towards the Dean's stall to declare loudly, 'I never did like you, Mr Dean, nor your bloody daughters!'

a difficult farewell to her mother, Peggy and Mark, not yet two years old, made their way to Canterbury. Alfred met them with the news that Court's had given him the sack.

The firm had been forced to lay off staff, and the part-timers were the first to go. The Dellers' weekly income, consequently, slumped to three pounds. It was barely enough to pay their landlady, with hardly anything left over, and before Alfred had time to begin looking for another job a far graver event occurred: France fell, and the remnants of the British Expeditionary Force struggled home through Dunkirk.

At last the fact of war hit Canterbury. Until now there had been air raid warnings and an occasional haphazard bomb from single aircraft. There were next to no anti-aircraft defences. Now, plans for the evacuation of women and children were put into effect. Amongst the first to go were the boarders of the cathedral choir school. With their headmaster, Clive Pare, they were transferred to Par, in Cornwall, where they would function as a school for the rest of the war. And within a few weeks of rejoining Alfred Peggy was ordered to assemble Mark, one suitcase, food to last one day, but no drinks of any kind, and report early one morning to Canterbury railway station.

She found herself amongst a seething crowd of women and children. At nine o'clock evacuation officials herded them into railway carriages and locked the doors. There were no corridors. As they chugged slowly along some circuitous route to an unknown destination, the reason for the ban on liquid refreshments became apparent. For the women and children of her compartment at least, Peggy proved the saviour of the day. With supreme foresight she had given up a bit of her valuable luggage space to pack Mark's 'potty'.

London had been raided severely that day, and the train went by the roundabout route to avoid it. As night fell it entered Oxford. The carriage doors were unlocked and the distressed occupants released. Billets had been arranged for them, but the London raid had sent a flood of evacuees scattering to the closer provincial towns. Many had reached Oxford and had filled the billets before the Canterbury contingent arrived. Harassed officials and voluntary workers herded the exhausted women and crying children into a schoolroom for the night. There was still nothing to drink and the lights could not be put out, so the children went on milling about and sleep was impossible. Again, Peggy was able to do the trick. She created such a fuss that tea was produced and the lights were put out.

As she tried to sleep she saw the dark shape of someone stooping over her. An official whispered to her to pick up Mark and come with her. Outside they were put into the charge of a policeman and led through the streets to a house. The policeman thundered on the door. It was getting on for midnight. When the householder and his wife appeared the policeman informed them that Peggy and Mark would be lodging with them for six weeks. Then he vanished into the night. No doubt comforted by the thought that they might have had a mother and twelve children thus delivered to their doorstep, the couple welcomed her in. She still believes that the whole thing had been quickly organised by the reception authorities because they could tell a trouble-maker when they saw one.

Back in Canterbury the entire atmosphere has changed. The Cathedral organisation had changed, too. Dr Knight had been conscripted into the R.A.F. The Precentor, Canon Poole, a fine musician whose duties had hitherto been more concerned with choir discipline and administration than with the music, had been placed in charge, with the sub-organist, William Harvey. The choir itself was much reduced. There was normally a double choir of boys at Canterbury—twenty-four boarders and twenty-four day boys. With the boarders gone to Cornwall and some of the day boys evacuated there remained a total of five lay clerks and six or seven little boys. Canon Poole had to supply the missing tenor part on the cantoris side, and often had to answer himself in versicles and responses. Gradually local boys came in, and within a couple of years they had twenty-four boys, so that services were maintained right through those hazardous times.

'We had the time of our lives', Canon Poole recalled. 'Being on the brink of eternity made it much more fun being here.'

Deller found himself constantly called upon to take over the top line in anthems and help out the boys. It added further to the interest of his work. He was still eager to sample all musical experience, and knew how much more of it still awaited him. He was twenty-eight, but he had still not heard the term 'countertenor'.

A few weeks after his twenty-ninth birthday his call-up papers came.

He had abhorred violence from boyhood. Even before the war he had been sufficiently moved by the world news to write and tell his father he felt himself to be a pacifist. The Sergeant had responded in a way characteristic of men who had never paused to doubt their own conception of duty, manliness and courage: he answered that, while he could not approve, he understood. Coming from an uncompromising old soldier, whose haven of contentment was the drill hall and whose reading was the drill manual, the letter moved Alfred very much. Not all people, he was to find, would sympathise so readily.

He had his first unpleasant experience of what pacifism could mean to others when, early in the war, he went to Canterbury Labour Exchange to register for military service. There were young men milling around him, making a lot of noise, and he had to shout to make the clerk hear that he wished to register as a conscientious objector. He was overheard. A chorus of jeers broke out. Violence seemed possible, and he was ushered quickly out of a back door. He was spotted and followed some way by cat-calling men.

He had never discussed pacifism with Peggy. She knew broadly his views, and approved of them. He had no illusions about what Hitler and his kind stood for, and fully recognized its evil. At the same time he saw, as he had done all his life, that fighting was evil in itself. He understood the motives of his friends who went willingly to join the forces—but for him these motives were not valid.

What depressed him was the belief that so many of those who submitted to conscription and meekly took up arms were pacifist at heart. At a personal level, every man should know his vocation, whether for peace or for war, and should be unafraid to follow it. Totalitarianism, whether Fascist or Communist in kind, was the supreme example of what he termed 'the disease of secularism—life apart from the worship of God through Jesus Christ', which he believed had brought the world into its present tragic state. But, on the evidence of many of their economic and political practices, the democracies, too, were anything but free of the disease. Mankind could only hope to cure itself by spiritual attitudes; war would spread the germs.

Looking back in later years, he affirmed, 'That was my attitude, and very pompous it all sounds. But, in its essence, it is still my belief. If I had had to die in the war it would have been my wish to die creatively, by which I mean to die offering no resistance. To die having killed someone myself would have been to die destructively, and I saw every act of destruction as being against the good of mankind. The destruction of Hitler and his movement purged a great deal of evil from the world; unfortunately, though, the evils of what I called secularism are still with us today. This is the enemy all men should be taking up arms to fight.'

This was his case when he appeared on 4 October, 1940 before a tribunal sitting at Bloomsbury County Court in Great Portland Street, London. The combination of his views, his profession of lay clerk at Canterbury Cathedral and his willingness to undertake non-combatant duties convinced the members of his sincerity. He was registered as a conscientious objector and instructed to join the Air Raid Precautions organization or find work on the land.

He had already given some passive support to the war effort. Since Dunkirk he had been giving one night each week as a stretcher-bearer, helping to shift casualties being dispersed through Canterbury. It had brought him into contact with A.R.P. workers, whose duties, it seemed to him at that uneventful stage of the war, involved sitting about in shelters playing darts and cards by the hour. He chose the land.

The problem now was to find a farmer close enough to Canterbury who would take on a conscientious objector, totally unskilled at farm labouring, and give him full freedom to carry on with his cathedral duties. He found the Labour Exchange sympathetic and almost miraculously helpful. At Sturry, only three miles from Canterbury, a Quaker family named Headley were farming. An enquiry brought the reply that they had no vacancy, but would be pleased if Mr Deller would call on them. He went by bus, accompanied by Canon Poole, who knew the Headleys slightly. The elderly couple and their two sons were friendly and sympathetic, but repeated that they had no job to offer. The interview ended and the visitors were invited to step in for 'a simple farmhouse tea'. Disappointed, Deller began to refuse, saying something conventional about not wishing to impose himself. He was surprised to hear Canon Poole murmur, 'Don't be silly, Alfred. Go in and sing for your supper. They're interested in music.'

So they went in and sat down to the 'simple' tea, which proved to be an enormous cold collation, the centre-piece of which was a dish holding the largest number of boiled eggs Deller had ever seen in his life. All his life, food was the surest reviver of his spirits.

He began to talk, and, as usual, everyone was content to listen to him. In due course, Mr Headley leaned across the table to ask if he would care to sing. Although full of eggs, home-made bread, tea and other luxuries of those days of rationing, he agreed readily.

Canon Poole remembered: 'I played for him on a not very competent upright piano. I think he sang Purcell's *Music for a while*: at any rate, it was something he did very beautifully. In my opinion, it so captivated Mrs Headley's heart that he was offered a part-time job as a farm hand. If he had not taken a cup of tea on that farm at Sturry that afternoon, the chain of events might never have occurred which led to his becoming recognized as the countertenor of the century.'

Certainly, if the Headleys had not taken him on, he might have had great difficulty in finding any other farm where his situation would be so suited to his carrying on his cathedral duties to the full. Even so, he was in for no soft passage. His wage was to be ninepence an hour. He would have to bicycle to Sturry every morning in time to start work at seven. At nine, he would have to pedal hurriedly back to Canterbury for 9.30 Mattins. After Mattins, back to Sturry for another hour's work before lunch; an hour or two more labouring after lunch, then back to the cathedral for Evensong. On Friday, his free day from the cathedral, he worked at the farm all day, and at especially busy times such as harvesting and threshing he had to be excused from choir duties altogether.

'It was back-breaking when I first started. I'd never done such hard physical work before, and then there was the cycling to and fro, always behind time. But before long I was as fit as a flea, and loved it all.'

He wore colourful shirts of red, orange or blue, made up by Peggy from old casement curtains. Outdoor life darkened his skin, which, with his black hair, earned him the reputation amongst the villagers of being a 'bloody eyetalian' prisoner-of-war, and there was some talk of messages being flashed to the enemy by him.

There was no time to change before dashing into the cathedral. His cassock covered his farm clothes, gum boots and all. His nearest squeak was when he tore into the choir stalls with seconds to spare before the start of a special service for the visiting Russian Primate.

'I fell into my stall, barely able to speak. A manuscript part I'd never seen before was thrust into my hand. The words were in anglicized Russian, a chant of welcome, or something. Within a minute of throwing my bicycle down outside I was singing everything from Vladivostock to Smolensk I could think of. Anyway, it worked.'

Peggy, meanwhile, was moving around Oxford. After she had been eight weeks at her first billet her hosts reminded her that the period for which they had been required to take her had expired a fortnight before. Instead of applying to the appropriate officials, she simply walked down the road to a large house where she knew there were no evacuees, rang the bell and announced that she had arrived. There was a nursery for Mark, and a nanny, whose room Peggy had to share. They stayed for some weeks, until Peggy got word that an uncle and his family had taken a house at Lambourn, Berkshire. After lonely months amongst strangers who resented their presence she was glad to take Mark to live amongst her cousins and their children.

For some time Alfred had been lodging in Canterbury in the home of a fellow lay clerk, Reg Tophill. Now, he moved into closer relationship with a couple with whom he had been developing a friendship since not long after his arrival in the city. Geoffrey Keable was rector of the ancient church of St George the Martyr, in Canterbury, where Christopher Marlowe had been christened in 1564. When he had appointed Keable in 1933, Dr Hewlett Johnson informed him that since he himself had time only to deal with national affairs it would be up to Keable to 'stir up Canterbury'. This the new rector and his wife, Gladys, set about doing with a vigour which promptly brought roars of reactionary wrath dinning in their ears. Charges of Bolshevism, blasphemy and un-British activities were hurled. In fact, what the Keables and an eager group of church members were doing was almost precisely what Alfred Deller and the Christ Church Young Group had been trying to achieve; to bring the church out of its isolation to play a responsible part in the social and political affairs of the world.

With no qualifications, but guided by the celebrated example and teaching of Conrad Noel, vicar of Thaxted, Essex, the St George's Group, or Canterbury Lambs, as they sometimes called themselves, set out to associate themselves with more progressive movements in the city with the aim of creating a favourable climate of Christian public opinion. Geoffrey Keable gained election to the local unemployment committee. His wife stood three times for the Labour Party at municipal elections, though more for propaganda value than from an expectation of being elected. The many slums still remaining, despite all that had been done by a former Dean, Canon Bell, provided another obvious target. The Quakers, small in number but influential, made it possible for the St George's Group to convene a meeting at which the Canterbury Churches Housing Fellowship was founded to recondition old houses and give constructive advice to the city council. It functioned valuably and successfully for a number of years.

The Group looked beyond the boundaries of Canterbury for objectives. It helped the Peace Council and the Spanish Aid Committee, getting up meetings, displaying posters, distributing literature, collecting money and clothing for refugees. It 'adopted' a Spanish child. One year the St George's Sunday School children shared their Christmas party with Spanish children, the next year with little Austrian Jewish refugees.

They were not essentially pacifists. The question, could Christianity be reconciled with any kind of violence at all, was a frequent theme of their debating sessions. The group's aims were to combat Fascism, to fight every kind of apathy, and, first of all, to drag the Church out of the precincts and into the streets. They made many mistakes, of both tactics and tact. The more controversy they could provoke, the more publicly-uttered abuse they could attract, the more encouraged they felt to press forward. The mayor and corporation were invited to attend St George's for a civic service on St George's Day. A councillor replied publicly that it would be an affront to the ratepayers for them to accept. Before the war had begun it was already being put about that the St George's Group were working to soften the will of the populace to resist if Germany should ever attack, a strangely illogical charge to level at a visibly anti-Fascist body. There was an even more distasteful rumour that the children of St George's Sunday School were being taught to spit on the crucifix.

Geoffrey Keable recalled: 'In so many parishes the question is constantly arising, "Is it worth while dividing a congregation, arousing hostility, emptying the pews, losing money?" One must judge for oneself; but it was clear that no new life could have come into St George's without those early reverses. We made many staunch friends, both within and without the boundaries of the parish. Conrad Noel showed us how to look for the working of the Holy Spirit in bodies outside the confines of the church. We found it true that many who thought they had repudiated the teaching and worship of His followers were yet unconsciously carrying out Christ's spirit in their lives. We argued and discussed and worked, afterwards worshipping together in devotions before the Blessed Sacrament. We argued with atheists on the existence of God. We read papers on the social meaning of the Sacrament. We thrashed out the question, can a Christian be a pacifist? We believed it was blasphemy to pray for peace unless we also did all we could to bring it nearer. St George's worked and prayed in the belief that a live church group must learn about events of our time and use its small powers to help shape them. Look-

ing back, one regrets many mistakes, but chiefly that
we were not able to do more. At any rate, when the
storm burst in 1939, there were some who were awake
and understood.'

The Keables' and St George's most controversial
days were over when Alfred Deller got to know them,
but the work and beliefs of the energetic young group
brought an immediate response from him. Although he
'belonged' to the cathedral, his desire to be associated
with an Anglo-Catholic church had brought him to St
George's. He paid his first visit to the Keables on
Easter Sunday afternoon, 1940, having been warned
by someone, 'They're all mad.' He arrived at the rectory
in his Sunday suit, a sober pin-stripe. He rang the front
door bell; there was no response. In the distance he
could hear laughter and someone playing a recorder.
After a suitable pause he rang again; no one appeared.
Diffidently, he walked round the house to the garden.
A large and eccentric looking group was huddled
around a priestly figure wearing a cassock. A barefoot
recorder-player, sitting astride a garden swing, spotted
the stranger and called to the priest. 'Ah!' exclaimed
Geoffrey Keable, hastening over to him. 'Do have a
fig sandwich!' It was the beginning of what Deller
looked back upon as six of the happiest and most
rewarding years of his life.

He started cautiously, though. 'My first reaction in
approaching a church and a priest, both of which I
knew were unpopular with the local Establishment,
was to keep my guard up. At Christ Church we had
been a very small minority group out of a large and
fashionable congregation. We had been tolerated because the rector had approved of us. At St George's I
found almost the entire congregation involved in this
attempt to apply Christianity to economics and politics.
I felt I ought to be wary, but it only lasted for a moment.
When I met Geoffrey Keable, and saw how his rectory
was an open house and centre of the community, it
made a tremendous impression on me. I could see that

for these people the liturgy was the centre of life and the thing on which all their activities were based. Then there was the intellectual side. Gladys Keable organized the Marlowe Club to read plays and hold discussions. It probably all sounds absolutely hair-raising and arty-crafty, but it wasn't. The local milkman was one of the leading figures. There were some chaps from the railway, some schoolgirls, an architect. Some of the older people were in it, as well as we young ones. Everything we did had something in common with what I felt, and it influenced me immensely.'

The rectory was known to the Group as the 'George and Dragon', and they came and went as they pleased, day or night. 'In those days there were no organizations like the Samaritans or Alcoholics Anonymous, and so forth, so all sorts of people would come to us for help,' Geoffrey Keable explained. 'From time to time there would be an ex-criminal living with us, or a homosexual, or someone just out of a gas-oven or an asylum. They were totally accepted as part of what was in effect a large Christian family.'

Some weeks after Peggy had left Canterbury, Gladys Keable was evacuated to Guildford. Her husband proposed to Alfred that they set up a bachelor 'chummery' at the rectory, which they did, with the milkman as third member. It was an hilarious interlude, with two such 'natural buffoons', to quote Mrs Keable, as Alfred Deller and her husband in close proximity. For each of them the endless private jokes, the bandying of surrealist quips, and Alfred's mimicking of the cathedral clergy served as a safety-valve to ease off the pressure of hard work and frustration.

Alfred was working long hours at two occupations, each of which, in its way, demanded all he had to give. He had also resumed his stretcher-bearing duties one night a week at the Kent and Canterbury Hospital. He found these varied duties satisfyingly worth-while, but he was ever conscious that time was slipping away for him.

He was nearing thirty, and almost penniless. He had attained a place in a notable choir and was filling it with distinction, an achievement which at one time would have satisfied all his ambition. Now, he was impatient to go further and make an individual name in music. If his chance to do so did not arrive before long it would be too late: he would have no future except that of an ageing cathedral alto.

By now, Peggy was anxious to return to Canterbury. The daily woman who 'did' for the bachelor household at St George's was not altogether satisfactory, and Alfred suggested that Peggy should come and live with them and take over the duties. This was agreed and she and Mark moved in. The job was no sinecure. She never knew in advance whether two people or half a dozen, several of them strangers, would sit down to the next meal. However many there were, the same rations had to suffice. More than once, one small 'Woolton pie'* intended for four or five would finish up feeding a dozen. But she was glad to be back with Alfred, and although large numbers of enemy aircraft could be watched almost nightly passing over Canterbury towards targets further inland there was little to suggest that a woman with a small child and another baby due in a few weeks' time would be safer anywhere else.

31 May 1942 was Alfred Deller's birthday. It was a Saturday. Gladys Keable had just left the rectory after one of her periodic weekend visits from Guildford. Another visitor was Peggy's mother, in Canterbury for the first time and feeling rather out of place in such uninhibited company, but doing her best to live up to the high spirits around her.

It had been a gorgeous day. Alfred had sung at Evensong and then assisted Geoffrey Keable to give a concert of gramophone records to an audience of soldiers. In the afternoon Peggy had taken her mother

---

*A wartime concoction of vegetables and pastry, named after the Food Minister, Lord Woolton.

walking all round St George's parish, with its narrow streets of ancient houses clustered under the towering cathedral.

A few hours later there was no parish left. At one o'clock in the morning of Trinity Sunday, instead of passing Canterbury by as usual, the massed bombers struck.

FIVE

Mrs Lowe, sharing a room with Peggy and Mark, listened apprehensively to the drone of approaching aircraft and roused Peggy, who reassured her that the siren went every night as planes passed over heading for London. Only if 'Tugboat Annie', the hooter which would sound the imminent warning, were heard would they need to do anything.

The planes were nearer. There was no anti-aircraft fire. Mrs Lowe could hear a sort of tinkling noise against the sound of the bombers. When Peggy listened she could hear it, too. At that moment 'Tugboat Annie' began to blare. The door burst open and Alfred came in, crying, 'They're here!' The tinkling sound had been the patter of incendiary bombs raining on the roofs and roads of Canterbury.

The women leaped from their beds and Peggy grabbed Mark. Seconds after she had lifted him up a fire-bomb plunged through the ceiling and fell in the centre of his cot. Alfred stayed to put it out as the women went downstairs, to sit in a corner of the hallway which seemed to offer most safety. They chose well. Other incendiaries came through the roof and into various rooms, to be dealt with promptly by Alfred and the rector. When the high-explosives began to fall soon afterwards a bomb exploded some twenty-five yards away, demolishing several houses with the force of its shock waves and blowing the rectory door across the hall. The sheltering women and child were untouched. The house next door was in flames; the gas main in the street was burst and flaming; the express-train roar of high-explosive bombs seemed to be heading straight towards them, while incendiaries continued to make the night brilliant. The one member of the household who expected to live through that night was Mark, aged three. At the height of the noise and confusion the little old lady from the burning house next door ran into the rectory, terrified. Mark greeted her, 'Hello, Mrs——! Will you have a sweetie?' Their fear was never quite so great after that.

Several hundred aircraft had converged on Canterbury simultaneously. From 1 a.m., thousands of incendiaries had been dropped to light the target, starting raging fires in the town centre, with its mass of ancient, tinder-dry houses. Bombing with high explosives followed and continued until 2.15 a.m. The whole historic area of twenty-four acres from Watling Street to Burgate Street and from Rose Lane and Butchery Lane to Lower and Upper Bridge Street was blazing. It would continue to flare up at intervals for a week. Three-quarters of St George's Place was burnt out. The historic old church was gone, except for the tower, which remains today in the centre of the rebuilt area.

When the 'All Clear' sounded and it was safe to go into the street, a horrifying spectacle greeted the St George's household. Flames, sparks and smoke towered into the sky so thickly that it was impossible to see whether the cathedral still stood. According to hurrying passers-by it had been levelled to the ground. There was too much to be done in the shattered parish of St George's to allow them time to go and find out the truth. It was not until next morning, when Alfred cycled to report for duty at the hospital, often dismounting to carry the bicycle through piles of smoking debris, that he saw that the cathedral still stood. It was virtually undamaged. There had been direct hits on buildings immediately beside it, including the chapter house, the library, and part of The King's School. Many incendiaries had fallen on the cathedral roof, only to be pushed straight off by the long poles of firefighters stationed there, high above the ground, thanks in great part to the foresight of the 'Red Dean'. He had also had the idea of preparing the cathedral crypt as a safe shelter, capable of holding hundreds of people from near-by houses. Although St George's parish had been wiped out in an hour, the loss of life had been mercifully small, for most of the householders had taken advantage of the cathedral's ancient sanctuary.

When the news reached the Headleys, at Sturry, they sent word at once insisting that the Dellers and Geoffrey Keable come to the farm to stay. There was nothing left to be done in Canterbury, which swarmed with firemen and salvage workers from places as far away as Woolwich. Mrs Lowe returned home, leaving the three Dellers and Geoffrey Keable to move out to Sturry, where they thankfully settled down for an early night.

During the day, barrage balloons had been rushed into the area and now ringed the city. When the bombers returned that night, few were able to get through. Frustrated, they dropped their bombs on the outlying areas, one of which was Sturry. The rectory refugees found themselves for the second night running in the thick of a combined incendiary and high-explosive raid.

In the space of an hour some 1,500 fire bombs fell on the Headleys' property. One 'Molotov Breadbasket' container full of incendiaries landed squarely on the centre of the roof of the farmhouse, splitting on impact, as it was designed to do, and sending its bombs scattering down the front and back of the building. Incredibly, not a spark touched the roof, but the whole farmyard seemed to be alight. A haystack was flaming like a torch, so brightly that the crosses on a low-flying bomber's wings were clearly visible. Straw lying about the yard was blazing, cars and equipment were burning with oily smoke and a stench of rubber. Some bombs crashed through the corrugated iron roofing of the pig-sties and the air began to ring with the animals' terrified screams.

Bertram Headley, Geoffrey Keable and Alfred, wearing pyjamas and steel helmets, dashed from the farmhouse towards the sties. Deller remembered: 'Several times we saw planes coming and had to go flat on our

faces till they were past. When we reached the sties there
was pandemonium. There was one great sow, screaming
her head off, with the straw burning all round her. I
kicked open the door and she ran out. Just outside the
sty was a pile of mangelwurzels. As soon as she saw
them she went straight up and started to eat them,
though she'd been terrified nearly to death a moment
before. I was scared stiff myself, but I had time to take
it in as a reassurance about the extent of animals' feelings
of fear or pain.'

Although the damage to the farm had been miraculously slight, there was not accommodation for the
Dellers to remain there for any length of time. With her
second baby's birth drawing near, Peggy evacuated
herself again, this time to Little Chart, near Ashford,
where an elderly relation of the Headleys had an ancient
house made out of two joined cottages. The old lady
was kindly, but impractical. Opening a larder door,
Peggy found it full of old and crawling food. She
slammed the door shut and never opened it again; but
the thought, whenever she passed that way, of what
was happening in the larder, together with the general
creepiness of a house with two front doors, two back
doors and two staircases, so affected her that she
panicked. Telephoning her mother that she would
rather risk the hit-and-run raids on Hastings, she went
home. On 21 October, Simon was born there.

After the birth Peggy returned to live with Alfred
and their children at Sturry, where the Headleys had
cleaned up and furnished a disused oast cottage for
them. The Dellers paid seven and sixpence a week rent,
and got it all back in free provisions, including fruit
they could pick from their windows. They shared the
cottage with innumerable mice which nonchalantly
drank from the cat's dish and ran all over baby Simon,
with no apparent ill-effects. They were preferable to
maggots.

After several months the Dean offered the family the
use of the choir school, which had stood empty since

the evacuation of its pupils. They moved in with the few oddments of furniture they possessed: it was the first time they had had their own things about them. It was a comfortable home. In the kitchen was an old Aga cooker, which neither of the Dellers had any idea how to use. Popping in from the Deanery next door, where he was living, sleeping and working in one small study, the Dean recognized their plight. 'Umm, we'll soon get that going,' he said, slipping off his black jacket and kneeling in his gaiters before the fire-door. 'Umm, pass me some wood and paper.'

In Alfred's view: 'A lot of hard things have been said about the late Dr Hewlett Johnson, and I know how disliked he was by many people, both in the Precincts and out in the world at large. I can only say how extraordinarily kind he was to us. He helped in every way he could, from lighting that Aga to insisting that we put Mark and Simon down to sleep in one of the bunks kept for his family in the crypt. Whenever "Tugboat Annie" sounded we would dash over from the choir school to the crypt, and invariably we'd find the Dean there, gaiters and all, organising things. Whatever time of the day or night it was I never once saw him out of full dress. We thought he must go to bed in his gaiters, because he could never have done up all those buttons in time to get over to the crypt as quickly as that.'

When Geoffrey Keable returned to Canterbury on a visit he found the Dellers moved from the choir school to the warden's house at St Augustine's, the Anglican training college, which was also virtually empty. They lived rent-free in return for Peggy's cooking for the sub-warden. Later, they occupied one enormous room in the college itself, with Peggy's cooker at one end, Alfred's piano at the other, and Simon playing trains in the middle. With his own church destroyed, Geoffrey Keable had taken acuracy at Harrow, refusing to accept another living of his own in order to remain titular rector of St George's and so save the parish from extinction. The bombing had done nothing to destroy the St George's Group, which continued to meet when and where it could; rather, in Geoffrey Keable's words, 'It had bound us together for life.'

It was 'business as usual' at the cathedral, too. 'Like another celebrated establishment,' in Canon Poole's words, 'we never closed.' * The bombing had shattered most of the glass, making the main body of the building too exposed for the daily offices to be sung there. The eastern crypt was chosen as an alternative. The very day after the main attack a solemn procession set off from the Treasury towards the crypt, led by the Vice-Dean, old Canon Crum, and Canon Poole. As they moved along a side aisle they saw a workman on a high ladder, knocking out fragments of glass remaining in a window. Canon Crum called to him, 'That's right, you do your job and we'll do ours.' They filed on down into the crypt and proceeded to say Matins, amongst the dust and rubble, with a single candle to light them. Deller found the services in the crypt especially moving. 'The whole thing was alive with emotion. You felt you were in the catacombs, and so much nearer to a full understanding of what Christianity was all about. I think, for me, that was the nearest I have ever come to it.'

Canon Poole was determined that the cathedral music should continue. Sung services were resumed in the crypt, still with a depleted choir of five lay clerks and a dozen or so day boys, with an additional two or three volunteers at weekends. The crypt remained in use as a bomb shelter, and it was while sitting down there one night during an alert that Canon Poole first read the manuscript of a new work he had managed to commission for his small choir. It was Michael Tippett's *Plebs Angelica*.

Poole had first taken real interest in Tippett's work

---

*The proudly advertised boast of the Windmill Theatre, London, which continued its non-stop variety and girlie shows throughout the Blitz and the war.

early in the war after running two miles through blacked-out Canterbury to reach a radio set in time to hear the Second String Quartet. Its affinity with the polyphony of the great age of English music impressed him enough to make him write to the composer, asking him to write a Mass for Canterbury. Tippett replied that he could not do this, pointing out that as one of the *pagani* he could not sincerely compose a Christian work; and if he were to leave the ranks of the *pagani* he would be abandoning them. To Canon Poole's mind, 'This was a profoundly Christian statement, the statement of a man of integrity and honesty for which I have ever since honoured Michael Tippett.'

To Poole's proposal that he should, at least, write something for him, Tippett suggested that a work much less personally committed than a Mass would be an anthem, and suggested a fragment in honour of St Michael from Helen Waddell's collection of mediaeval Latin lyrics. *Plebs Angelica* was the result, a double-choired motet first performed by the Canterbury choir in the crypt and given its first public performance at Canterbury by the Fleet Street Choir. Deller found it a work of great beauty and interest. He little realised that the commission to the then little-known composer was going to bring about the transformation of his own career.

Tippett was thirty-six. Not many months earlier he had finished serving a three months' prison sentence for refusing to assist the war effort. Now, with his oratorio *A Child of our Time* just performed for the first time, he seemed about to break out of obscurity and achieve a major position in British musical life. Much of his work outside composition had been in the adult educational field. In 1931 he had first become associated with Morley College, then London's chief centre for adult education. Its redoubtable principal, Eva Hubback, had engaged him to work with an orchestra of unemployed musicians. Quite early in the war a land-mine had destroyed most of the college, with the exception of the entrance hall, some classrooms and the small music room dedicated to Gustav Holst, the most eminent of the college's musical directors. His successor, who also taught at Westminster School, had left London for good when his pupils had been evacuated, and Mrs Hubback asked Michael Tippett to replace him.

It was a labour of love, with scarcely any pay, but an admirable opportunity for a young composer and conductor to get on in his profession. He could work with an already good amateur choir, varying between thirteen and eighty members, which Tippett and his associate, Walter Goehr, improved to the point of excellence. Their free Sunday night concerts became notable in London, attracting crowded audiences of young people, British and foreign servicemen and G.I.s to the various halls in which they appeared.

Since before the war, Tippett had been fascinated by the music of Purcell and the Elizabethans. Most recitals by the Morley College Choir included examples of their works, but one difficulty recurred constantly. Purcell had been a countertenor, and he had written for the voice in many of his bigger works. Knowing that there had been no possessor of a countertenor voice for a century and a half in Britain or anywhere else, Tippett had to look for a compromise. Instinct told him that to engage a conventional male alto, out of some choir, perhaps, to sing Purcell would prove anything but successful: as unsatisfying artistically as it would be to use a female contralto for the essentially masculine countertenor part. One experiment he tried was to perform the big *Ode for St Cecilia's Day* with groups of his Morley College singers taking the solo parts in unison. It was partially satisfactory and gained a notice in *The Times* affirming that there could be considerable public interest in such hitherto little-heard works. Tippett saw clearly, though, that the problem of the extinct countertenor stood inexorably in his way.

In the course of their correspondence about the Mass

for Canterbury, and the substituted *Plebs Angelica*,
Canon Poole had mentioned to Tippett that the cathedral possessed an alto of rare accomplishments and
urged him to come and give him a hearing. The opportunity did not offer itself immediately, and the suggestion drifted into the background. It had not been the
first time that Joseph Poole had written to established
musicians about Alfred Deller. Nothing had ever transpired: the position of a cathedral alto, however good,
was no recommendation at all in the musical profession's eyes. Scope for the voice as a solo instrument
simply did not exist. Deller himself was realist enough
to recognise this; and yet he too had for some years
been studying, purely for his own interest, the neglected
glories of Henry Purcell's work. There had been little
chance to do anything practical about it. His many
duties kept him far too busy to think of recital engagements, even if, in evacuated and bomb-torn Canterbury,
there had been any such opportunities offering. But he
had not yet given up hope of some day making a mark
of his own in music; and the more he saw of Purcell's
music, the likelier it seemed that it could be through
this that he would make it.

Once more, Fate lent a hand. At this very moment,
when the Purcellian reflections of both Michael Tippett
and Alfred Deller had come almost to the point of
converging, the two men met. By an extra coincidence
it was Gladys Keable who helped to bring them finally
together, and that by utter chance.

She had taken the opportunity of a brief holiday in
Cornwall with some other members of the St George's
Group, and was now returning by train with one of the
girls, Jo Roberts, when a group of men who could
only be musicians entered their compartment. In accordance with tradition there was no conversation
between the two parties and eventually the train reached
Plymouth, where one of the musicians, 'a very interesting-looking person', in Mrs Keable's recollection, got
out. The journey was resumed. Again, for all the hours

to London no conversation passed. Then, with perhaps half-an-hour to go, Jo began searching for her hat. This broke the ice. All the others helped her search, until the hat was at last unearthed, crushed, from beneath the musicians' luggage. Conversation now flowed freely. What was Mrs Keable reading, the musicians wanted to know? The mediaeval mystics. How interesting! Brief discussion of this topic. Then, from her in return, who had been that interesting-looking man who had got out at Plymouth? Oh, Michael Tippett. Perhaps she mightn't have heard of him, though. Very *avant-garde*. Just out of prison.

Gladys Keable had heard of him, and knew that Joseph Poole had written to him about Alfred Deller. She told them. 'Get him to write again,' advised one of them, and introduced himself as Antony Hopkins.

Joseph Poole did write, and Tippett replied that, as he was coming to Canterbury to hear the Fleet Street Choir give the first public performance of *Plebs Angelica*, he would be pleased to hear the alto sing. In Michael Tippett's own words: 'I was at that time wrapped up not only in Purcell, but in the Elizabethans and all the early English school. One of my heroes was Orlando Gibbons, so the first thrill of that visit to Canterbury was to enter the practice room in the choir school, which I found to be almost unchanged since Gibbons himself was there in the sixteenth century. It was in those evocative surroundings that I heard Alfred Deller sing Purcell's *Music for a while*. It was not a very good arrangement of it; but for me, in that moment the centuries rolled back.'

SIX

This was the voice Michael Tippett had only dreamed of ever finding, and which Alfred Deller had only begun to realize he possessed when, studying and singing in Canterbury Cathedral some of the works of William Boyce, he had noticed that his alto part was always designated counter- or contra-tenor.

The question, what is a countertenor?—or when is an alto not an alto?—has been debated again and again, without, it seems to the present authors, ever having been answered with definitive clarity. Having broached it, we must not shirk from making the attempt: we suggest that a countertenor is, quite simply, a male alto of exceptional brilliance and flexibility.

Tippett has similarly defined the voice: 'The countertenor is a male alto of what would be regarded now as exceptional range and facility. It was the voice for which Bach wrote many of the alto solos in the Church cantatas; and Purcell, who himself sang countertenor, gave to it some of his best airs and ensembles. To my ear it has a peculiarly musical sound because almost no emotional irrelevancies distract us from the absolutely pure musical quality of the production. It is like no other sound in music, and few other musical sounds are so intrinsically musical.'

When asked to define it himself, Alfred Deller was forthright.

'Two questions have been put to me constantly during my years as a professional singer. The first, which is of a personal, not to say intimate nature, I leave to the imagination. The second is, when did you decide to become a countertenor? This is rather like being asked when I decided to be born. I had no choice in the matter: it just happened. I joined my parish choir at eleven with a good strong voice, a good ear and a good memory. I became solo boy, and by the time I was fourteen had made a local reputation as a soprano. I continued to sing soprano solos in the annual performance of the *Messiah* until I was sixteen. I had no yodelling difficulties during the voice-changing period, and when the organist asked me to continue in the choir as an alto I made no conscious adjustment to my voice production. I couldn't. I only knew the one way to sing. It would have been less embarrassing to have sung a sort of baritone, which I would have been capable of doing, though in an undeveloped and inexpressive way. When, eventually, I met Michael Tippett I was still singing alto and calling myself an alto. He said to me, "When you sing for me, I shall give you the old English classical name for your voice, which is countertenor." And that is how I became a countertenor.'

When Tippett revived the term countertenor he was paying tribute to the uniqueness in his time of Alfred Deller. By his great gifts, combining peerless technical facility with consummate artistry, Deller retrieved the countertenor voice not from extinction, but from eclipse. In the two centuries of that eclipse the tradition of male alto singing had never ceased. It had merely been driven underground—if one may use the term to describe its confinement to the cathedral choir and the barber shop quartet, as opposed to the solo opportunities offered by the theatre and the concert platform. In confirmation of his youthful feeling that, somehow, he was a 'marked man', Deller was to be able to leave the anonymity of the choir stall to fashion a career of his own which would gain him world acclaim. It is no denigration of his gifts, or the way in which he used them, to suggest that he was fortunate (or 'marked') in the coincidence of several things: Michael Tippett's need for just such a voice as his; the twentieth-century revival of interest in the music of Purcell and his contemporaries, in reaction against the Victorian ro-

mantics who played a large part in pushing the countertenor further into obscurity; and the inauguration of
the B.B.C. Third Programme, which was to bring
Deller, and the countertenor voice, to international
notice and admiration.

No alto of Deller's quality had made a mark indivi-
dually during the past two centuries, and it is unlikely
that one has languished unknown. It also seems un-
unlikely that any future alto, calling himself countertenor and making a career as a soloist, will equal Deller's
fame. He may be matched some day for artistry and
virtuosity; but his place as pioneer is unassailable, and,
together with his gifts, assures his uniqueness. Save
for a difference in ages—and forty-odd in the sixteenth
century was not far from the fifty-plus of today—
Thomas Coryate, the English traveller visiting Venice,
might have been writing of Deller:

> Of the singers there were three or foure so
> excellent that I think few or none in Christen-
> dome do excell them, especially one, who had
> such a purenesse and (as I may in a manner
> say) such a supernaturall voice for sweetnesse,
> that I think there was never a better singer
> in all the world, insomuch that he did not
> onely give the most pleasant contentment that
> could be imagined, to all the hearers but also
> did as it were astonish and amaze them. I
> alwaies thought that he was an Eunuch,
> which if he had beene, it had taken away some
> part of my admiration, because they do most
> commonly sing most passing well; but he
> was not, therefore it was much the more
> admirable. Againe it was the more worthy
> of admiration, because he was a middle-aged
> man as about forty years old. For nature
> doth more commonly bestow such a sin-
> gularitie of voice upon boyes and striplings,
> than upon men of such years. Besides it was
> farre the most excellent, because it was

nothing forced, strained, or affected, but came from him with the greatest facilitie that ever I heard. Truely I think that had a Nightingale beene in the same roome, and contended with him for the superioritie, something perhaps he might excell him, because God hath granted that little birde such a priviledge for the sweetnesse of his voice, as to none other: but I think he could not much. To conclude, I attribute so much to this rare fellow for his singing, that I think the country where he was borne, may be as proude for breeding so singular a person as *Smyrna* was of her *Homer*.

The tribute to there being 'nothing forced' is interesting. *Falsetto* is an unhappy term, as the late Davidson Palmer expressed:* 'The term falsetto is a most misleading one, and its indiscriminate use has been mischievous in its extreme. The man who invented it has much to answer for. He has caused right to be mistaken for wrong, and wrong to be mistaken for right. He has made what is false appear to be true, and what is true appear to be false. Had it been his supreme desire to do all the injury in his power to the male voice of his succeeding generations, he could not, by the exercise of the utmost ingenuity, have devised means better calculated to accomplish his purpose. Falsetto exists and it should be used.'

In other words, there is nothing false about falsetto. How can there be? It exists, is produced without artificial aid. The 'singularitie of voice' so admired by Coryate almost certainly owed something to falsetto, as did that of Alfred Deller, who explained it thus:

'There are generally recognized to be two types of countertenor voice. The first, and more usual, is where the fundamental voice is baritone or bass, and the head-voice, or so-called falsetto, is developed to the maximum

---

*In his *Manual of Voice Training* (Joseph Williams—now Galliard Ltd—London).

range. My own voice is of this type. You produce this
head voice naturally, and you work on it as you would
on any other voice. But, if you wish, you can still sing
off the chest, so to speak. Purcell was a countertenor
of great ability; he also sang bass in the Chapel Royal
choir.

'The other type of countertenor is essentially a high
tenor who can either dispense with falsetto entirely,
or uses it for the top fourth or fifth of the compass,
without perceptible break. Some people say this is the
true countertenor; others, that it isn't countertenor at
all, but merely a very high, light tenor. Certainly, some
singers one hears who are billed as countertenors seem
to be just tenors with exceptionally high range.

'All in all, it's a most confused subject, about which a
great many vague theories have been propounded. The
one thing that is clear is that there is nothing to be
ashamed of in using and developing the falsetto extension to one's natural range. I agree with Lilli Lehmann,
who said, "Most male singers, tenors especially, consider it beneath them, generally indeed unnatural or
ridiculous, to use the falsetto which is a part of all male
voices. They do not understand how to make use of its
assistance, and of its proper application they have not
the remotest conception".'

Much of the modern neglect of falsetto may be due to
the cult of the ringing tenor who, in accordance with
one of the many dubious conventions of Italian opera,
must attack his high notes at full bellow, or be derided
for a ninny. Falsetto was valued by earlier generations
of Italian singers; even the *castrati* used it to extend their
range, and Farinelli's incredible ability to span three
octaves certainly owed something to it. One of Pietro
Francesco Tosi's observations reads, 'A diligent Master,
knowing that a male Soprano, without the Falsetto, is
constrained to sing within the narrow Compass of a
few Notes, ought not only to endeavour to help him
to it, but also to leave no Means untried, so to unite the
feigned and the natural Voice, that they may not be

distinguished; for if they do not perfectly unite, the Voice will be of diverse Registers.'

The distinction between the 'feigned' falsetto and the 'natural' castrato is a nice one, indeed.

The origins of falsetto are unknown. It is enough to know that men capable of singing falsetto existed in music's earliest days, and could sing with a facility and understanding which boys could not match. A great deal of early music was 'high' in character and included parts for one or more countertenors, of whom there must have been no dearth. Women's voices were not permitted in church music, so that all this considerable amount of music was sung by men and boys. One part they sang was the Discantus, a roving accompaniment to the 'straight' plainsong of the tenor. Another was the Contra-Tenor, lower than Discantus, which wove its way round the tenor, singing 'against' it: the hyphen helps explain its purpose in that role. There were two labels for contra-tenor: Altus and Bassus. In his *History of Music*, published 1776–79, Dr Burney says, 'In early times of counterpoint, human voices of different compass, occasioned by age, sex, and natural organ, were classed and divided into four distinct kinds, at the distance of only a third above each other, which the Base, or F clef placed from line to line expressed. The lowest of these was called the TENOR, the next CONTRATENOR, MOTETUS the third, and TRIPLUM the highest, or TREBLE, of which term this was the origin.' By the late fifteenth century, under the influence of the Sistine Chapel, the four parts had resolved themselves further into Cantus, Altus, Tenor and Bassus, the Altus still being known as the Contra-Tenor. In the following century it was de-hyphenated and anglicized into countertenor.

The seventeenth century was the countertenor's heyday. It was the heyday, too, of English music, and each owes much to the other. Michael Tippett says, 'I know of nothing comparable whatsoever to the music of the English Restoration. Nothing in any other country's music can surpass, in my view, this great flourishing under Purcell; and Purcell wrote much of it especially for the countertenor voice because history compelled him to. Cromwell had driven choral music out of the church, so that, by the time of the Restoration, there were no boys' voices being trained. Purcell had to train any sopranos he needed. It took him many years to get the tradition flowing again, and it was not until almost the end of his life that he could find boys' voices good enough to achieve the effects he wanted. Meanwhile, he used countertenor, tenor and bass for piece after piece, from the most delicate and intricate to those great odes and massive verse anthems, all calling for a great degree of virtuosity.'

Purcell himself was a better countertenor than most. When he took part in his new ode, *Hail, bright Cecilia*, at its first performance at Stationers' Hall, London, in November, 1692, the correspondent of the *Gentleman's Journal*, doubling as court correspondent and music critic, noted the 'incredible graces' with which he endowed the aria *'Tis Nature's voice*.

During his exile, Charles II had heard some impressive singing in Continental chapels: some of it, certainly, by Italian *castrati*, some, perhaps, by Spanish singers trained by the unrecorded and long-lost methods by which many falsettists of great skill are rumoured to have been produced. In 1679, Charles summoned one of the leading English countertenors, John Abel (or Abell), newly sworn a Gentleman Extraordinary of the Chapels Royal, and ordered him to go to Italy, learn all he could, and, it is said, at the same time show the Italians that they did not have the monopoly of good voices. On 24 January 1682, John Evelyn recorded, 'After supper came in the famous treble, Mr Abel, newly returned from Italy. I never heard a more excellent voice, and would have sworn it had been a woman's, it was so high, and so well and skilfully managed.'

Abel may have brought back more than mere hints on better singing. He was receiving worth-while payments of bounty money from the royal purse; not, it is suspected, as a form of bursary, but as reward for his activities as a spy.

When William and Mary succeeded to the throne in 1688 the payments ceased abruptly and Abel was dismissed from the Chapel Royal on suspicion of Romish leanings. He was exiled to the Continent, where he had the resource to travel widely, singing to his own lute. His outstanding voice and whimsical manner made him extremely popular wherever he roamed; except, perhaps, at Warsaw, where he refused to sing before the Court. This situation was soon resolved when Abel was seized, pitched into a chair and suspended over the bear-pit, with the threat that it was a case of sing or be lowered. He said afterwards that he had never sung better in his life.

He was allowed back to England and published a collection of his songs, prefaced by a judiciously worded poem:

> After a twelve years' industry and toil
> Abell at last has reached his native soil
>
> Not that he vainly boasts of bringing home
> The spoils of France, of Italy and Rome,
> Or thinks to please the Judges of the town
> From any other climate than his own,
> But humbly begs since foreigners could raise
> Your admiration and receive your praise.
>
> That he with some advantage may appear
> And bring English pleasure to an English ear.

He was still singing in 1716, when well over sixty, and was said to have some secret means of preserving his voice.*

Abel's most celebrated contemporary was Francis Hughs (or Hughes). Burney wrote of him, 'Mr Hughes had been a favourite singer at concerts, and between the

---

*Alfred Deller was still singing at 67.

acts of plays. For several years he was assigned the part of first man, in the first opera that ever was performed on our stage in the Italian manner. His voice was a countertenor, as we are told in the *dramatis personae* of *Thomyris*; and indeed, as the compass of his songs discovers. He continued to perform the first part till the arrival of Valentini, after which no further mention is made of him either in opera or concert annals.'

A further opera, *Arsinoe*, was produced at Drury Lane on 27 January 1705, with the express intention of introducing singing of the Italian style to the English stage. Thomas Clayton, whose enterprise this was, declared, 'Though the voices are not equal to the Italian, yet I have engaged the best that were to be found in England; and I have not been wanting, to the utmost of my diligence in instructing them.'

Arsinoe proved popular enough, even with its admittedly unremarkable cast, to encourage the production in 1706 at Drury Lane of another opera in the Italian style, *Camilla*. Many of the same singers were engaged, including Hughs. Whether he realised it or not, by appearing in such presentations Hughs was helping to bring about the eclipse of the countertenor. Late in 1707 it was revised, and Hughs once more sang, but this time not as leading man. He had been displaced by Valentini, the alto *castrato*, one of two Italians singing in their own language while the rest of the cast sang English. Valentini's singing, though by no means a great example of the *castrato's* artificial, yet compelling virtuosity, was enough to set the public appetite astir for more. It was a novelty with which no countertenor could compete. Hughs recognised as much, and retired to the uncompetitive haven of the Chapel Royal, where he sang for another thirty-six years until his death.

Burney wrote the countertenor's epitaph: 'But before a character is given of the great foreign singers who arrived here after Italian opera was firmly established in this country, it is but justice to say something of the English singers, who were able by their performance to excite curiosity, give pleasure, and set censure at defiance, when the opera was in its infancy, and regarded by some as an idiot, and by others as a shapeless monster.'

As we have seen often enough in our own time, the musical theatre in England is as susceptible as the rag trade to fashionable change. Music-hall succumbed to revue: musical comedy and escapist operetta were swept clean from the stage by the virility and social awareness of the 'musical'. So it must have been with the coming of the *castrati* at the beginning of the eighteenth century. Nothing like them had been encountered before. Their combination of brashness, flamboyance and mysterious non-sexuality added up to a considerable fascination. Their voices seem to have possessed a bewitching unearthliness. Their virtuosity must have been dazzling.

Their origin is hidden in antiquity. There have always been, and still are, natural eunuchs. Singing beside boys and falsettists they made useful church choristers, being invariably less unruly than the former and generally more accomplished than the latter. They faded from the European scene in the Middle Ages, reappearing again in the fifteenth and sixteenth centuries when Papal ears began to tire of the shrill cries of the Spanish soprano falsettists who had established the *a cappella* style, with elaborate and often florid textures beyond the powers of boys and ordinary falsettists. The return of the eunuchs coincided with, and no doubt owed something to, the rise of Italian opera. Opera in the Italian style has been one novelty which has endured, though in some cases less on the strength of the works which comprise its repertoire than on the skill and personality of generations of singers who have been content to use those tried and trusted works as vehicles for their own talents and conceits.

Italian opera and the *musici* or *evirati*, as the *castrati* were also widely known, were made for each other. A contemporary wrote, 'Their timbre is as clear and piercing as that of choirboys and much more powerful;

they appear to sing an octave above the natural voice of women. Their voices have always something dry and harsh, quite different from the youthful softness of women; but they are brilliant, light, full of sparkle, very loud, and with a very wide range.' Just the thing, in fact, to please Italian audiences; and it must be admitted, to please audiences wherever in due course they arrived. In Rome and many other places, women were not permitted on the operatic stage until the nineteenth century. They were not much missed with the *castrati* to fill the bill. These exotic creatures, as feminine, often, as any woman, and far more accomplished singers, were adored by both the male and female factions in their audiences, off the stage as much as on. Their physical shortcomings (induced during childhood by means of scalding hot baths, to promote near insensibility, and a quick operation with knife or pincers) made them safe playthings for ladies of high fashion, who could afford to dally with them to the limit without fear of an unlooked-for outcome; while gentlemen whose tastes inclined towards their own sex could hope for nothing more voluptuous than a young *castrato* of the type Casanova observed during a visit to Rome in 1762:

> We went to the Aliberti theatre, where the castrato who took the prima donna's role attracted all the town. He was the complaisant favourite, the *mignon*, of Cardinal Borghese, and supped every evening tête-à-tête with his Eminence.

> In a well-made corset, he had the waist of a nymph, and, what was almost incredible, his breast was in no way inferior, either in form or in beauty, to any woman's; and it was above all by this means that the monster made such ravages. Though one knew the negative nature of this unfortunate, curiosity made one glance at his chest, and an innexpressible charm acted upon one, so that you were madly

in love before you realised it. To resist the temptation, or not to feel it, one would have had to be cold and earthbound as a *German*. When he walked about the stage during the *ritornello* of the aria he was to sing, his step was majestic and at the same time voluptuous; and when he favoured the boxes with his glances, the tender and modest rolling of his black eyes brought a ravishment to the heart. It was obvious that he hoped to inspire the love of those who liked him as a man, and probably would not have done so as a woman.

Another who evidently did not care which sex he attracted had been encountered by Casanova some years earlier in a café:

'An abbé with an attractive face walked in. At the appearance of his hips, I took him for a girl in disguise, and I said so to the abbé Gama; but the latter told me that it was Beppino della Mamana, a famous *castrato*. The abbé called him over, and told him, laughing, that I had taken him for a girl. The impudent creature, looking fixedly at me, told me that if I liked he would prove that I was right, or that I was wrong.'

No such scandalous propensities marred the character of the greatest *castrato* of all, Carlo Broschi, known always as Farinelli. Farinello is Italian for rogue; yet for all the adoration he earned, both for his singing and his looks, especially from women, he seems to have lived the intrigue-free life of a dedicated artist. He is the only *castrato* known to have been of noble birth. That a nobleman should have allowed his son to be castrated at all is singular in itself. It may have been necessitated by an illness, and the child's father, a bit of a rogue himself by all accounts, perhaps decided to make the most of the misfortune by having him trained as a singer.

He was sent to Naples when very small to study under Nicolo Porpora, one of the most noted singing-masters and composers of the great age of the *castrati*. The life

The Professor.

Peggy Deller.

Early celebrity (with the late Desmond Dupré).

n Boughton Aluph Church.

The Raconteur.

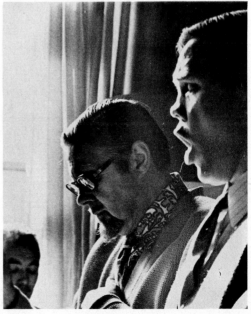

The Duettist (with Mark Deller).

The Recording Artist.

The Conductor.

The Last Year.

Sergeant Deller, Alfred's father, his wife and Alfred.

The Jester.

Possession.

As Oberon in Britten's 'A Midsummer Night's Dream' (1960)

of an apprentice *castrato* was harshly disciplined, but at the same time sufficiently lacking in supervision to lead to the youth's corruption by predatory men or women. The curriculum was unrelenting, consisting of at least six to eight hours of study a day, including voice-training, deportment, speech, counterpoint, harmony, composition and the playing of an instrument, generally the harpsichord.

Farinelli made his debut in Naples at fifteen, and first appeared in Rome two years later. Burney heard him at this time and illustrated the boy's astonishing powers by retailing the story of a duel:

> During the run of an opera, there was struggle every night between him and a famous player on the trumpet, in a song accompanied by that instrument; this, at first, seemed amicable and merely sportive, till the audience began to interest themselves in the contest, and to take different sides; after severally swelling a note, in which each manifested the power of his lungs, and tried to rival the other in brilliancy and force, they had both a swell and shake together, by thirds, which was continued so long, while the audience eagerly awaited the event, that both seemed to be exhausted; and, in fact, the trumpeter, wholly spent, gave it up, thinking, however, his antagonist as much tired as himself, and that it would be a drawn battle; when Farinelli, with a smile on his countenance, shewing he had only been sporting with him all the time, broke out all at once in the same breath, with fresh vigour, and not only swelled and shook the note, but ran the most rapid and difficult divisions, and was at last silenced only by the acclamation of the audience. From this period may be dated that superiority which he ever maintained over all his contemporaries.

He continued in this vein for nearly ten years, captivating his audiences by sheer virtuosity and personal charm, until, visiting Vienna for the third time, he was offered some shrewed advice by no less a critic than the Emperor Charles VI. Burney, who had it from Farinelli, recounts:

His Imperial Majesty condescended to tell him one day, with great mildness and affability, that in his singing, he neither *moved* nor *stood still* like any other mortal; all was supernatural. 'Those gigantic strides, (said he); those never-ending notes and passages *(ces notes qui ne finissent jamais)* only surprise, and it is now time for you to please; you are too lavish of the gifts with which nature has endowed you; if you wish to reach the heart, you must take a more plain and simple road.' These few words brought about an entire change in his manner of singing; from this time he mixed the pathetic with the spirited, the simple with the sublime, and, by these means, delighted as well as astonished every hearer.

This, then, was the complete artist who arrived in England three years later, in 1734. Burney waxed ecstatic:

Every one knows who heard, or has heard of him, what an effect his surprising talents had upon the audience: it was extasy! rapture! enchantment!

In the famous air *Son qual Nave*, which was composed by his brother, the first note he sung was taken with such delicacy, swelled by minute degrees to such an amazing volume, and afterwards diminished in the same manner, that it was applauded for full five minutes. He afterwards set off with such brilliancy and rapidity of execution, that it was difficult for the violins of those days to keep pace with him. In short, he was to all other singers as superior as the famous horse Childers was to all other running-horses; but it was not only in speed, he had now every excellence of every great singer united. In his voice, strength, sweetness, and compass; in his stile, the tender, the grateful, and the rapid. He possessed such powers as never met before, or since, in any one human being; powers that were irresistible, and which must subdue every hearer; the learned and the ignorant, the friend and the foe.

Sir John Hawkins recorded, 'In the city it became a proverbial expression, that those who had not heard Farinelli sing, and Foster* preach, were not qualified to appear in genteel company.'

The most famous tribute of all was the cry of a fashionable lady in one of the singer's audiences, 'One God, one Farinelli!'

The older *castrato* Senesino, so much employed by Handel, was in London at the time. Neither of the two singers had heard the other, and simultaneous appearances kept them from doing so. Then, at last, both were engaged to sing in *Artaserse*, a composite entertainment with music by a number of hands. The spectacle of the two greatest soloists the world had known upon the same stage quite overcame the orchestra at the first rehearsal: they sat gaping at Farinelli's brilliance and forgot to play. By the time the piece was ready for its first public presentation even Senesino was ready to acknowledge his colleague's gifts. Playing the part of a chained captive, Farinelli so melted Senesino that the latter forgot he was the furious tyrant and ran across the stage to embrace his victim rapturously.

The *castrato* craze was at its height, with results often familiar enough since. The *Gentleman's Magazine*

---

*James Foster, D.D., the Baptist, whose vigorous sermons at Paul's Alley, Barbican, and evening lectures at Old Jewry, were regarded by the *beau monde* as the height of fashionable entertainment.

observed, 'So engrossing are the *Italians*, and so pre-judiced the *English* against their own country, that our Singers are excluded from our very Concerts; *Bertolli* singing at the Castle, and *Senesino* at the Swan, to both their shames be it spoken, who, not content with monstrous salaries at the Opera, stoop so low as to be hired to sing at the Clubs!'

Farinelli spent three years in England, during which time rival managements frenziedly cashed in for all they were worth on the *castrati*, to the inevitable detriment of operatic standards. He would have stayed on indefinitely if the enterprising Queen Elizabeth of Spain had not thought of inviting him to sing to her husband, Charles V, who had for years been in the grip of melancholia so severe that he could neither attend to his affairs nor take any pleasure in living. Knowing that the King would not consent to hear the singer, the Queen arranged for him to do so as if by accident. It worked perfectly. Farinelli sang in another room; His Majesty 'overheard' him and was captivated. He offered the singer a salary of more than two thousand pounds a year if he would remain at court and give his exclusive services. Farinelli, who must have valued security above the hurly-burly of popular fame, accepted. He may have had other ambitions, such as political power, for he was soon interesting himself in a wide range of matters, from irrigation to horse-breeding, and was listened to at court. He paid for it all by having to sing every night to an audience restricted to the King and Queen and their intimate circle. He told Burney that these recitals invariably had to include the same four songs. After performing them nightly, and no doubt subjecting them to every sort of variation, for ten years, even Farinelli must have exhausted their possibilities. At any rate, they kept him from England.

After a heyday of some sixty years the fashionable interest in the *castrati* waned. Richard Leveridge, a bass who had sung falsetto alto in many English productions of Italian opera, ceased to use his falsetto except to burlesque the Italians. In similar reaction against the effeminacy it had encouraged by so idolizing it, the English musical audience turned in righteous reaction to the massive choruses and virile heroes of Handel, who, since *Deborah* in 1733, had dropped the *castrati* in favour of tenors and basses. He still wrote for an occasional countertenor—for instance, David and Joseph in *Joseph and his Brethren*, 1704—but he was now using *women*, and sometimes in male roles, an ironical example of gynandromorphism.

The *castrati* were gone—before long, they would be gone for good in Italy also. Behind them, the golden glories of seventeenth-century music lay in neglect. The dwindling band of countertenors could look neither to stage nor concert platform for opportunity. There remainded the church. But in 1772, visiting Brussels, Burney recorded, 'I was glad to find (at Ste Gudule) among the voices two or three women who...proved that female voices might have admission in the church without giving offence or scandal to piety, or even bigotry. If the practice were to become general, it would, in Italy, be a service to mankind, and in the rest of Europe render church-music infinitely more pleasing and perfect.'

Women had found their way into the choirs of Protestant churches in parts of Germany in the time of Bach, who had been rebuked for including his cousin (who became his first wife) and, later, his second wife amongst his singers at Arnstadt and Leipzig. They would soon infiltrate the choirs of Protestant churches in England, though it is only recently that they have penetrated cathedral fastnesses. The hitherto unknown female contralto would make her (to the already-deprived countertenor) sinister appearance. 'Permit me,' wrote a reader of the *Musical World* in 1836, 'to draw your attention to a situation in which myself, and others who have the misfortune of being denominated countertenor singers, are placed by the introduction of female contraltos in most of the festivals and concerts instead of the legitimate altos. For instance, not one of us is engaged at the forthcoming festivals at the Exeter Hall...'

Thus, by approximately the end of the eighteenth century, the countertenor's occupation was all but gone. It is small wonder that, listening to Alfred Deller in Canterbury that day in 1944, Michael Tippett should have felt the centuries roll back.

SEVEN

The centuries having rolled back, Michael Tippett, Canon Poole and Alfred Deller turned to discussing how the long-lost voice of the solo countertenor could best be reintroduced to the musical public. Tippett remembers the conversation well, 'because it developed into a frightful argument between Poole and myself and the deputy organist as to whether I should join the Christian church. Their view was that, as a member of the church, you were better placed to communicate sympathetically with the public at large. I took a composer's view that, with so many of my fellow men not inside the church, it was a limiting factor. However, when we'd discussed all that at great length, we returned to the question of "launching" Alfred Deller. I wasn't a concert promoter. I only had Morley College, where everything was done on a shoestring, so there was no money available. We decided to make a start by fitting him into one of the Saturday evening chamber concerts in the Holst room there.'

The concert took place on 21 October 1944. The hall was full, but it only held some two hundred people. The programme included Tippett's own *Plebs Angelica*, a piano sonata by Antony Hopkins, some Bartók and some Handel. Deller took part in two verse anthems by Purcell, *O sing unto the Lord* and *My beloved spake*, and sang again the solo with which he had so impressed Tippett at Canterbury, Purcell's *Music for a while*, this time in a new version made for him by a recent acquaintance, Walter Bergmann. A lawyer in Germany before the war, Bergmann was one of several talented, foreign-born musicians such as Walter Goehr and Matyas Seiber who had collected around Tippett at Morley College. Others included Norbert Brainin, Peter Schidlof, and Siegmund Nissel—three young refugee string players who had been educated in England, and who, with Martin Lovett, became the Amadeus Quartet. As well as the refugees, who worked in factories, there were young English medical rejects, like John Amis and Antony Hopkins, and young women, like Hopkins's wife, Alison Purves. So Morley College music went from strength to strength. Small and large groups of its performers appeared in halls and art galleries in evening and lunchtime concerts. Perhaps the principal single feat of this dedicated collection of professionals and amateurs was to rediscover and record Tallis's 40-part motet *Spem in alium*, composed for eight five-part choirs.

Bergmann was one of this team of enthusiasts; and it is his edition of *Music for a while* that Deller preferred to use from that time, and made a sort of signature tune connected with him all over the world. He could scarcely have made a happier choice than this haunting song, with its splendid ground bass, which Sir Jack Westrup* considers, 'apart from Dido's lament, the most satisfying, in technique and expression, that Purcell ever wrote.'

On the last day of the year, at an afternoon concert in the Friends' House, Euston Road, where an audience of more than a thousand could be accommodated, Deller made his true debut. The occasion was promoted to raise funds for the Morley College concerts. Tippett conducted. The programme comprised Buxtehude's *In dulci jubilo*, the Bach *Magnificat*, *Plebs Angelica*, and Purcell's *Ode for St Cecilia's Day, 1692*, the last and greatest of the four odes in which Purcell had displayed the instruments of music contending in turn for Cecilia's favour. Deller's singing, especially in the florid, Italian-style recitative *'Tis Nature's Voice*, which Purcell himself had sung with such 'incredible graces' at its first performance, was a revelation.

In Walter Bergmann's words, 'Suddenly there was Purcell again.'

---

*In *Purcell* by J.A. Westrup (Dent, London, 1937).

It was true. Purcell, the greatest glory of English music, had not suffered wholly from the eclipse of the countertenor voice upon which so many of his works depended for satisfactory performance: even with this subtracted, more than enough remained. Yet, in common with most other composers of his time and before, very little of him had been left visible above the flood waters of that Romanticism which had so exactly suited the taste of the long Victorian age and nearly half of the following century. The first stirrings of revival had come in 1876, when the Purcell Society had been founded with the intention of publishing a definitive edition of his works, the majority of which still only existed in manuscript. A handful of specialists and enthusiasts, aware of the riches they alone could appreciate, had worked on quietly into the twentieth century, against the day when, as it must, fashion would swing. But mere fashion could not set a full-scale Purcell revival going. Unlike his colleagues in letters and art, the composer can rarely communicate directly with his public; especially the composer who has been dead for well over a century. He must await the arrival of a sympathetic interpreter of persuasive enough gifts.

Lionel Tertis raised the viola from an orchestral instrument of the second rank to a solo one of the first. Segovia brought the guitar from the *flamenco* cave to the classical concert platform. Kathleen Ferrier gave new standing to the contralto voice, and Maria Callas and Joan Sutherland a new look to the worn operatic repertoire.

It would be excessive to suggest that, in his almost unwitting rescue from oblivion of a voice-type which he had scarcely known he possessed, Alfred Deller single-handedly resuscitated Purcell also. It would not be fair to the Purcell Society, to Michael Tippett, nor to several other contributors to the Purcell revival. One of them, Sir Anthony Lewis, Principal of the Royal Academy of Music, who has been responsible for arranging and conducting many notable Purcell works which had seldom been performed since the composer's day, has given his assessment of Deller's part in the revival:

'He helped to open up a great repertoire of Purcell and Handel, not unknown perhaps to a specialized musical public, but not hitherto accessible in really professional presentation. That is to say, the obstacle in the way of performing those works requiring a virtuoso countertenor had been so great that allowances had to be made, compromises met, and this had an adverse effect on the whole status of the performance. Concert promoters, conductors and others with first-class standards to keep up steered clear of these works because they knew that there would be occasions during the performance when the standard would inevitably drop, due to the incompetence of the available alto soloist (or, worse still, female contralto substitute); and so the works never reached the most important platforms.

'Alfred Deller, by his first-class interpretation and unassailable technique, gave such promoters confidence to put on these works at the highest artistic level, bringing them off before a highly sophisticated and critical public. So, quite a number of works which had simply been regarded as historical relics, not normally accessible in the concert hall, came forward into the ranks of the acknowledged masterpieces.'

Deller assisted the Purcell revival, and the Purcell revival helped Deller. Perhaps the starting-point of the new momentum each gave to the other was the concert at Friends' House, though the brief notice in next day's *Times* did not mention him, singling out only Margaret Ritchie and Peter Pears for having sung 'confidently', while 'Not all the five solo voices in the Bach could be said to have reached the necessary standard.' The notice conceded in a back-handed way that 'on balance, a true enough idea was given of certain pages of incomparable music to explain the enthusiasm of a large audience.'

The enthusiasm, at least, was undeniable, even by *The*

Times critic. It was reaffirmed at several further concerts presented by Tippett and the singers and musicians of Morley College, at all of which Deller was invited to perform. One of the most important, from the point of view of the discerning type of audience it would be sure to attract, was at the National Gallery, one of the celebrated series which had done so much to keep English music-making alive during the war. Tippett had only one misgiving: there would perhaps be not half a dozen people in the audience who had ever heard a countertenor voice. The rest were in for something of a shock. There might be audible reaction enough to put the obviously nervous Deller off his stride and ruin this chance of making a telling impression. 'I decided to address the audience,' Tippett recalls. 'I told them that I was very pleased to present Alfred Deller, the possessor of this remarkable countertenor voice, and that I was pleased to hear from him that he was already training his two sons to sing, too. It seemed to do the trick. There were no murmurs when he started to sing, and he proved a great success.'

During this period he was enabled to reach an audience many times greater than the total of those who had heard him so far by being asked to broadcast. He entered broadcasting with a smoothness most artists would envy. There was no audition, no apprenticeship of brief recitals at unlikely hours of the morning. He was engaged straight away to sing the principal counter-tenor part (billed as alto) in a studio performance of *Hail, Bright Cecilia*, conducted by Constant Lambert. Other broadcasts followed in the B.B.C.'s domestic and overseas services.

Meanwhile, his work as a lay clerk at Canterbury went on. His concert appearances and broadcasts had to be fitted into the time off he could get from this and his farm work until released. He did not resent it. He had known throughout his time farmworking that, hard though he was having to toil, others were suffering infinitely more than he.

'My conscience never wavered, but my resolution did, especially during the time of the London blitz. I felt that I wasn't sharing enough in the general suffering, so I wrote to the Church Army, offering myself for duty at one of the refreshment stalls or reception centres they were running in the heart of London all through the worst of the bombing. They answered that there was no opening for me, but at least I felt some relief at having tried to do something more. When Canterbury was blitzed, and we found ourselves in the thick of danger at last, it was a sort of personal relief for me, terrible though it was.

'My conscience was never anything but clear about what I was doing. I was working as hard as I could at a useful job—two useful jobs. My family life was as disorganized as anyone's. I was living from pillar to post, and certainly making no money by remaining a civilian. Yet there would always be moments throughout the war when I would think, "By golly, those chaps in the Forces are making the real sacrifice." It was very comforting, though, to find that almost everyone I came into contact with was sympathetic to my position. There were a few unpleasant incidents. I received an anonymous letter, containing a white feather; and there were some cards—anonymous, of course. I still have one of them. It reads: "*Conchie Deller, Sturry. You are a coward, but you endanger your wife's life.*" There were one or two comments from acquaintances, during my first year as a conscientious objector, and a bit of ill-feeling within the family. But then it came round to harvest time on the farm. There were not enough of us to manage the work, and there was no casual labour to be had, so troops were sent to help us. They all knew they were coming to a Quaker farm, and that "conchies" would be around. I worked with those soldiers on the threshing machine, carried away stooks with them, and so forth, and made no bones about my position when we got talking. The heartening thing was that not only did they understand my point of view, but they seemed to share it. It seemed to me that most of them were pacifists at heart, as I believe most men are throughout the world today.'

Between the surrender of Japan, in August 1945, and his release from the farm in the following summer, Alfred, Peggy, Mark and Simon Deller managed to live together in Canterbury and enjoyed the first unbroken period of family life they had known since the beginning of the war. They were able to move from their one room in St Augustine's to a flat in a gracious Queen Anne house near by in Lady Wootton's Green, though Peggy found herself once more in surroundings with a touch of the macabre. The Dellers occupied the two top floors of the house. The ground-floor residents were twenty-five cats, many of them deformed. The owner of the house, a maiden lady, lived elsewhere and visited the house twice a day to feed the strays she had taken in. Otherwise, the animals lived quite alone, and the Dellers kept their doors firmly shut. It was, all the same, a house of great charm and attraction, which Peggy would have loved to have been able to buy and move into permanently. She and Alfred loved Canterbury. They had many friends. Wartime restrictions were beginning to lift and life was becoming at last more relaxed and enjoyable. Alfred's occasional broadcasts and concerts were bringing in some extra money. He was doing a little music-teaching in Canterbury schools, while Peggy was also managing to earn a little by working two evenings a week as secretary to the headmaster of the cathedral choir school. Then Deller's Fates decided the time had come for another phase in his life to begin.

He was cycling to the farm one morning when he met the postman, who gave him an envelope imprinted 'British Broadcasting Corporation'. Alfred opened it, and went straight back home to show Peggy the invitation to him to sing in the inaugural concert of the B.B.C. Third Programme on 29 September 1946.

The sender of the invitation was Anthony Lewis,

then a member of the B.B.C. Music Department charged with arranging the Third Programme's first concert plans.

'I first heard of Alfred Deller through Sir Steuart Wilson, who was Music Director of the Arts Council at the time. He knew I was hoping to include some of the big Purcell works in my arrangements, and wondering how I should get over the countertenor problem, and he came to tell me of a very remarkable countertenor he had heard at Canterbury. I managed to hear Alfred, and knew at once that it would, after all, be possible for me to put in Purcell's ode *Come, Ye Sons of Art* as one of the two major choral works in the inaugural concert. The work was hardly known, and, if Alfred had not come along, would probably have remained so.'

It was conducted by Sir Adrian Boult. Benjamin Britten had written a specially commissioned Festival Overture. There was Handel's *Music for the Royal Fireworks*, Vaughan William's *Serenade to Music*, Parry's *Ode on a solemn Music*, and Arthur Bliss's *Music for Strings*, conducted by himself. Lewis continues, 'It was a fine concert of fine music, but its most remarkable feature was the Purcell ode. Alfred sang the first countertenor part, and Lambert Wilkinson, a member of St Paul's Cathedral choir, the second. The effect of two artists who possessed such unexpected voices singing the duet *Sound the Trumpet* was simply sensational. It was a specially invited audience of the select musical public and all the critics, and there is no doubt that the impact of Alfred's extraordinary vocal quality and personal technique on them made that concert one of the turning-points in his career.'

The sensation is not reflected in the restrained notice from *The Times*, and neither Deller nor his fellow countertenor was mentioned by name, though there was some near-praise for them:

'Handel's "Music for the Royal Fireworks" followed. Purcell's ode *Come Ye Sons of Art* was too alike in scoring for it immediately to assert its individuality, though this little impediment was soon swept away on the entry of the voices, which included two countertenors. It was a revelation to hear the familiar duet "Sound the Trumpet" sung by voices of this unfamiliar timbre, for Purcell obviously intended the resemblance to trumpet tone to have the effect of happy allusion.'

Others made no bones about their enthusiasm. Concert offers began to trickle in. There was tentative talk of some recording. The B.B.C. offered more Third Programme broadcasts. The advent of the Third Programme, the first broadcasting service in the world to consist of a cultural content unfettered by the limitations of fixed timing or the need to compromise with the demands of a mass audience, had been awaited with as much interest abroad, especially in Europe and America, as at home. Deller's distinctive part in the impressive inaugural concert brought him at once to the attention of, literally, the musical world. It could only be a matter of time, dependent largely on the period it would take to sort out the cultural chaos left by the war, before he must be invited to perform in other countries.

Almost at their first meeting, Walter Bergmann had offered him two realistic pieces of advice. The first, intended to preserve his uniqueness and make himself less vulnerable to criticism arising from his choice of repertoire during the time it would take him to become established and independent, was to sing only music composed for the countertenor voice. The second, and less arguable, was to leave Canterbury as soon as possible for London, the essential base for his professional career. This latter counsel had been discussed between Alfred and Peggy, without so far being acted upon. Both were reluctant to give up the only real security they had yet achieved for another leap into the unknown and very likely hostile life of London. Now, however, the move was inescapable, if he were to pursue the promise of celebrity. The Canterbury choir was small, and offered no chance of his employing a deputy to stand in for him while he fulfilled another engagement. He was getting all the time off that he could be permitted, but needed much more. He would have to make a move, and to London. But where? As usual, the question was promptly settled for him. He applied for, and was offered, a place at St George's Chapel, Windsor, but there was no house available. Instead, he joined the choir of St Paul's.

The advantages would be considerable, as Bergmann, Tippett and all his other professional associates assured him. The choir of St Paul's Cathedral is the country's biggest, with eighteen vicars choral on the full strengh, divided into six countertenors, six tenors and six basses; and thirty-two boys. Deller recalled what Sir Steuart Wilson had once told him: 'The great advantage of being at St Paul's is that you never need be there.' There was much truth in it. The Anglican Church, in one of its more realistic attitudes, does not insist that its professional choristers be fervent, or even practising churchmen, a view which has brought only gain to Anglican church music. Many distinguished concert soloists have passed through the choir of St Paul's, helping to maintain its notable standard, adding an effective dimension to the offices of worship. At the same time they have justifiably lost no chance to further their secular careers. Consequently, a splendid substitution system had long existed when Deller joined. At Sunday services, except for five free days each year, all eighteen vicars choral were required to be present. On weekdays, only twelve were needed, allowing each man two completely free days. If a man was not free on a certain day when some outside engagement was offered him he could ask one of his free colleagues to stand in for him, and pay him for doing so. In addition, there was a list of 'authorised gentlemen', several of each type of voice, approved by the organist, who could be called upon by a vicar choral to take his place on up to forty occasions each year.*

This excellent system promised to benefit Deller more than any of his colleagues. Tenors and basses were in much greater demand for concert work than countertenors, and even so liberal a deputy system was sometimes strained by a rush of demands upon it. Of the six countertenors, it transpired, Alfred Deller was by far the most required for outside engagements, and seldom found himself asked to deputize for one of the others; while they, asked to take his place, were happy enough to accept his payment for doing so. It was, and is, an excellent system of musical patronage, benefiting both church and secular music and helping many professional singers to advance their personal careers. Without it, Deller's own career might have been retarded by several important years, and perhaps prevented altogether from reaching its heights. The St Paul's offer came at precisely the moment it was needed, enabling him to move to London without sacrificing the continuity of his choral work and the small but regular income it provided, while at the same time giving him the freedom to accept almost every outside engagement which came his way and to catch the chance of success and fame on the wing before the helpful novelty value of his voice could pass.

Grateful as he was for the appointment, the cathedral, through its Precentor, George Sage, a former Canterbury colleague, was delighted to be able to add him to its establishment. The Dellers, who had no capital with which to finance yet another change of home, were given a mortgage by the cathedral and luckily discovered that an uncle of Peggy's was about to move out of his house in Merton Park, Surrey, and would sell it to them. By buying directly from him they were able to save money on middlemen, so that the upheaval, if painful, was not ruinous.

---

*Vicars Choral are now required only to fulfil fifty per cent of their duties in person.

Peggy disliked the new house, loathed making the move, and was worried about the effect on Mark's education. He had been able to start attending Canterbury Choir School as a day boy. When Alfred mentioned this at St Paul's he was given the assurance that Mark would be taken into the choir school there instead. The last difficulty seemed to be resolved, and plans were made for the actual move to Merton. Then, a few days after they had arrived in their new home, they learned what no one had thought to tell them before, that Mark's entry into St Paul's Choir School would depend upon a voice and educational test. This was annoying, but not alarming, for Mark, whose voice was already promising, had passed his tests for Canterbury successfully. To his and his family's dismay, the St Paul's examiners declared that he had too small a voice, and refused him admission. *

It was the sort of challenge to which Peggy could, and can, be guaranteed to rise. Returning to Canterbury, she saw the choir school headmaster, for whom she had worked as part-time secretary, and told him of their determination that Mark should have the musical up-bringing for which he had proved himself fitted. Mr Pare sympathized, but pointed out that he had not managed to win a boarder's place, only a day boy's. Peggy asked if Mark could still attend as a day boy, if she could somehow arrange it. This was readily agreed, and she set off on round of day boys' parents, seeking someone who would take the responsibility of accepting a seven-year-old as a paying guest. It was no easy quest, but eventually a Mrs Newns agreed. Having won two rounds, Peggy still had one to fight. The choir school fees, plus the extra cost of board, were quite beyond their means, even anticipating a steady trickle of concert and broadcasting fees. She took a train to Hastings and went to see her mother.

*Nevertheless, he went on to become Head Chorister at Canterbury, and had voice enough to sing the leading role in an opera by Antony Hopkins for the Festival of Britain there.

'Look, Mother,' she said, 'if we find we can't pay Mark's school bill when it comes, will you guarantee us for a year while I go out and get a job to raise the money?'

Her mother agreed, but her help was never needed. Peggy went back to London and was able to find a job with the Town and Country Planning Association. It did more than save the financial situation: it renewed one of the Dellers' warmest friendships, for the woman who got her the job, and worked beside her, was Gladys Keable, who recalled:

'They were pretty poor. Mark was eight and Simon was four. Having fixed up the one in digs, Peggy had to pay housekeepers and neighbours and people to look after the other while she was at work. After a while she had to go away and organize Town and Country Planning conferences all over Britain, which made everything even more difficult. But I don't think she ever wavered. Alfred's life was his music, and that was how it was going to be. She was getting very little out of it herself. Music was not the whole of life to her, as it was to Alfred. She wasn't wrapped up in it, and I don't think she was happy in the completely strange circle of people Alfred's work had taken them into. She couldn't share his success, either financially or by being able to be with him; and yet I'm sure he owed a great measure of that success to what she did for him behind the scenes.'

The Archbishop of Canterbury, Dr Fisher (later Lord Fisher of Lambeth) was present at Alfred Deller's last Evensong. When it was over he took him aside and wished him well. The Dean followed suit, then the organist and choir. As he left the cathedral, Alfred broke down. The most rewarding years of his life were over. He was going forward to a place where he knew he was more than welcome, and where it would be his privilege and pleasure to sing in one of the country's finest choirs. From the way things were going, it should be only a matter of time before his name would mean a good deal, far beyond the limited territories in which he had so far moved. Yet, he sensed, nothing in his life would ever again be so cosily ordered, so intimately bound to the family and friends nearest to him. He might become famous, and make money and have things he had never been able to contemplate before; but he knew what it would cost him. He did not think of turning back. At thirty-seven he felt as much a 'marked man' as he had done at seventeen.

On the first day of 1947 he sang for the first time in St Paul's Cathedral.

EIGHT

Mary Deller died that year, in Canterbury Hospital, of cancer of the stomach. She was seventy-four.

With the coming of a second world war, the Sergeant's physical training practice had crumbled away irretrievably. It had taken him most of the years of peace to build it into something approaching prosperity. The splitting up of the family, with seven children leaving home one by one, had eased things by stages. The Sergeant had lost none of his energy with increasing years. His schools retained him year after year, businessmen of increasing sleekness and rotundity came to him for trimming down, children needing postural and remedial treatment were sent to him. The exercises he taught worked wonders with people—Paul Robeson's son amongst them—with asthma and other breathing disorders. He taught Baroness Orczy to fence (she was in her fifties at the time, and already famous as the author of *The Scarlet Pimpernel*, so presumably she did it for the exercise, rather than in pursuit of useful knowledge). The Deller household could afford to have everything delivered to it, and to pay the tradesmen by monthly cheque. The Sergeant gardened as hard as ever, though now for the love of it: he no longer swept the chimneys. Then a second war came and snatched away all they had achieved.

Once more, the old soldier could hope for no active military calling. Like any other civilian of no essential occupation on the Kent coast he had to pack up his things and go to an area where the brunt of the expected invasion could not fall. Regretfully, he took down from the parlour wall the plate with the coloured picture of Lord Roberts, the photograph of himself and his horse in India, the framed chocolate box which had been

Queen Victoria's Christmas present to the lads in South Africa. When the last of their family had left them, he and Mary, with great good sense, had made a complete break with the past, turning out all their old furnishings and starting afresh with new. The old war relics had stayed, though; and now, with no capital and their whole income gone at a stroke, the old couple were back to where they had been twice before, in their first days and again after the first war.

They took rooms in London. Deeply concerned for their safety, Alfred kept trying to persuade them to leave. They would not. The Sergeant had picked up a connection with a school and was earning a little. Then their two-roomed lodging received a direct hit. Alfred, who had been pulling any strings he could get hold of, hurried to London and brought them down to Harbledown, the ancient hamlet just outside Canterbury where Chaucer's last tale is told, and Lanfranc's leper hospital, founded 850 years ago, has become a cluster of almshouses round an astonishing Norman church. It was not easy to persuade the Sergeant to accept the almshouse Alfred's influence had obtained. His greatest fear was of losing his independence or relying on the charity of others, in which category he included any form of State assistance. But Alfred's persistence won and the Sergeant and Mary settled into their last and most charming home, with its pretty lattice windows and the big hedge for the Sergeant to clip as meticulously as he still trimmed his moustache. Looking from the window one winter's morning, after it had snowed all night, Mary saw the mantled tombstones, all round in the church-yard, and exclaimed, 'Why, they're like choirboys with their surplices on!' They accepted retirement and settled contentedly into a Darby and Joan eventide—though when victory was announced, it was Sergeant Deller, never mind his seventies, who went up the long disused steps of the belfry which had stood since before Magna Carta and got the Union Jack hoisted at the top.

But now, after fifty years of marriage, Mary was gone. She took the fierce old man's spirit with her, leaving him bewildered and lost. For all his well-intentioned tyranny, she had been the one who had really run things. In her quiet, accepting way she had been the mainstay, support and comfort of them all, the Sergeant included. In their last years together she had become the dominant one.

Though he had never realized it, none of them would miss her more than he. Left alone, still active but with all occupation gone, and denied by life-long refusal the solace of reading, he was a sitting target for the senile decay which proceeded gradually to overwhelm him. His remaining five years were ones of sad decline, but Alfred Deller always kept one memorable impression from almost the very end, in 1951. Visiting his father in a nursing home at Westgate-on-Sea, he sat waiting for one of the brief spells of lucidity in which the old man would recognize him and be able to exchange a few sentences before lapsing once more into meaningless rambling. Suddenly, the Sergeant burst into song. It was his old favourite, *Swing me up a little bit higher*. To his son's astonishment, the voice was a tenor of lovely, true quality.

'I'd never heard him sing like that before. His eyes were shining, and he sat, propped up with a pillow, and sang the old song, remembering every word, in this astonishing voice. That was the last time I saw him. He was buried near my mother, at Margate.'

Following the brief, sad family reunion occasioned by Mary's funeral, Alfred returned to London and the steady progress of his career. He had settled quickly into the new routine of St Paul's and was already receiving proof of its benefits to his concert career. He was now being asked to sing at festivals and performances far from London and to broadcast frequently. But if he took advantage of every chance his cathedral post gave him to further his own ends, he gave plenty in return. His influence on church music, both in performance and in repertoire, has been considerable. According to Canon Poole:

'He exposed the poverty of the cathedral alto, and persuaded people in charge of cathedral music to work to get more musical and more agreeable sounds in the alto line. I don't think even King's College, Cambridge, would have gone so far as to produce that perfect blending of the altos with the tenors and basses but for the example of Alfred Deller's voice. His influence on the repertoire has probably been more oblique. By playing such a part in the revival of the music of Purcell and the Golden Age through the medium of the Third Programme, he helped to shame cathedral organists into purging their repertoire of much music which, when looked at alongside such masterpieces, had been shown up as valueless. None of us realized just how valueless, until we got another standard of comparison, which Deller helped to bring us.'

'Until Deller, the alto was regarded as a sort of vice that one had to put up with,' Sir Jack Westrup adds. 'Many cathedral organists have groaned under the burden of their altos, particularly altos who grew old and did not become more pleasant with their age.'

Had women been admitted to cathedral choirs, it is possible that there would have been no alto revival for Alfred Deller to lead. Altos have kept their place not because of, but in spite of themselves; not because of their artistic value, but by tradition. His example has given incentive to more boys to develop a gift for an alto voice through into manhood, instead of shame-facedly letting it drop. No other countertenor of his stature has emerged as a result; but there is no doubt that the increased number or those who today sing countertenor in the concert hall, or alto in the cathedral, sing better because of him.

In 1948 he made yet another firm friend when Canon L. John Collins joined St Paul's as Chancellor. Canon Collins ('I was not quite so busy in those days as I am now') made a practice when in residence of joining the organist and some of the choir for coffee after services. Before long Deller and he had recognized much of themselves in each other and were taking their coffee tête-à-tête.

'We used to talk a lot of rather critical stuff about the cathedral singing. As Chancellor I had to do with the choir school, but not with the choir as such. Later I became Precentor and got to know much more of Alfred's musical views. They were very definite ones and we spent a lot of time discussing ways of improving the services. In fact, I always used to discuss things with him before I made suggestions to the music authorities, so that I could talk with some measure of musical authority myself. Many of the improvements that were made sprang originally from him. For instance, in services when we only had men singing, the practice had been to share alternate verses of the psalms between the choir and the bass soloist. It meant that if you happened to have your weakest bass on duty you were stuck with him as soloist. Alfred got me to have that altered, so that the verses were sung antiphonally, between the two sides of the choir. It was his idea to stop having the Amens played on the organ, and to start using settings by Byrd, Morley, Tomkins and others in addition to the eternal Ferial and Tallis for the versicles on saints' days. The outcome was that the services became much more musically agreeable, and at the same time more devotionally fitting. He impressed me as having a strong instinct for what was most appropriate. I put it down to his being not only a good churchman, but a Christian who understood deeply that his Christianity had to be worked out in everything he did in his life.'

If there is a single master key to any man's character, this is the one to Alfred Deller's, as, indeed, it is to Canon Collins's own. Another who shares Deller's instinct for action through Christianity and, with her husband, helped him to develop and express it, is Gladys Keable. 'Essentially, I think he still found that the faith he had been taught when he was young remained acceptable and valid for him, and he continued to base his life on it,' she says. 'He had a tremendous sense of the wholeness of life; that the whole experience is not one to be divided into separate compartments of religion, music, pacifism, politics, or anything else. In bringing out the whole beauty of music he was bringing out something that is a beautiful part of life, and of the Trinity; and so he did it as perfectly as he could, as an act of worship.'

It is a creed which leaves little room for compromise; and only the great artists and individualists can occupy their vulnerable position without compromising in some way. Though he had his moments of doubt, Alfred did not shirk to act out his pacifism to the full in wartime. Nor did he fail later to hold to his artistic beliefs in the face of all criticism. His voice, he well knew, was not to everyone's taste. There was nothing he could do, or wished to do, about that. Certain liberties of rhythm and phrasing which he insisted upon taking, and one or two mannerisms—'Dellerisms', they have come to be called—provoked varying degrees of annoyance in some of his hearers. The knowledge of this did not perturb him. There are few who have been associated with him, professionally or privately, who have not been able to regard his foibles as marks of his uniqueness, or, at worst, as amusing eccentricities; and almost every one of his critics has acknowledged his achievement and stature. More as man than as artist, he saw himself as imperfect in many ways; yet the few real hostilities he encountered did, at the time, outweigh all else and depressed him deeply. He was unable to remind himself that he was being criticized merely for some detail of performance, or for some personal shortcoming. It was as Alfred Deller, artist, man and Christian all at one, that he had incurred displeasure; and suggestion of failure in any single respect implied for him disapproval of the whole. For a brief moment, it undermined the foundations of his being.

Such criticism, however, was almost unknown to him at this time in the late 1940s when his career was still young and vigorously budding. His worries then were more tangible ones. Money was still very scarce. As well as the two boys, whose boarding-school education had to be paid for, there was now baby Jane. Freelancing, an insecure enough state in any profession, taxes hardest those who have come up from little or nothing: they know too well what awaits them at the bottom again. The spectre of financial calamity was never far from Alfred Deller's thoughts, even in his years of fame.

An invitation, which seemed to have been long in coming, to make a gramophone record for His Master's Voice proved to be unrewarding financially but immensely valuable in other ways. He sang *Music for a while* and *If music be the food of love*, both by Purcell in editions by Walter Bergmann, who accompanied him on the harpsichord. The disc caused a discernible stir in music circles and was followed with two more, again at 78 r.p.m. One was Humphrey's *Hymn to God the Father* and some Handel arias. The other was of two Dowland songs, *Flow my tears* and *In darkness let me dwell*. This time he was accompanied, unusually, on the guitar. It was played by another new acquaintance of his, Desmond Dupré.

Dupré had been playing the classical guitar from the age of twelve, having taken it up with the idea of somehow accompanying his mother, a violinist. He had been dissuaded from professional music and sent to read chemistry at Oxford. After graduating he practised as a chemist for some time before throwing it up for music. He considered himself a pianist for a while, then switched to the 'cello, which he studied at the Royal College of Music. At the college he became enthusiastic for old instrumental music and returned to his guitar in order to play lute music. He played one evening at a musical party, at which another guest was a fellow alto of Deller's at St Paul's, Duncan Thomson,

now Canon Precentor of Ripon Cathedral and headmaster of the Choir School. Thomson reported enthusiastically to Deller. Dupré was then living at his
brother's vicarage in Battersea, and arrangements were
quickly made for Deller to go there and try some
Dowland songs with him. The result so satisfied them
that they made the first of what would be countless
appearances together, and, soon after, the first of their
many recordings. *

The discovery of an artist with such understanding
and facility for lutenist music as Dupré added a further
dimension to Alfred Deller's art. His position as the
supreme living interpreter of Purcell was assured. He
was recognizably the finest cathedral alto of living
memory. Now he could show what he could do amongst
the neglected treasures of lute song.

English lute song—secular song to the accompaniment of the lute, played either by the singer himself or
by another—owed its origins to Europe. Lacking a
natural troubadour tradition of her own, England
subsisted thinly in the way of secular music until the
late sixteenth century on songs brought from abroad,
or on home-composed music to French and Italian
verses dealing chiefly with such emotional themes as
love fulfilled or unrequited. These sentiments were
ideally in tune with the great Elizabethan literary and
musical renaissance; and what Spenser, Sidney and
Shakespeare achieved with the sonnet, John Dowland
and Thomas Campion did equally gloriously with the
lute song. Dowland, in particular, was a virtuoso on
the instrument, unrivalled in Europe. Some idea of
the esteem in which he was held as performer and
composer can be had from the sonnet, sometimes
attributed to Shakespeare, written by Richard Barnfield
'To his friend Maister R.L., in praise of Musique and
Poetrie', in 1598, the year following Dowland's publica-

---

*Desmond Dupré collapsed and died in a train on his way to perform with
Deller in 1974. He was 58.

tion of his 'First Booke of Songes, so made that all the parts together, or either of them severally, may be sung to the lute.'

> If Musique and sweet Poetrie agree,
> As they must needes (the Sister and the Brother),
> Then must the Love be great, twixt thee and mee,
> Because thou lov'st the one, and I the other.
> *Dowland* to thee is deare; whose heavenly tuch
> Upon the Lute, doth ravish humaine sense:
> *Spenser* to mee; whose deepe Conceit is such,
> As, passing all Conceit, needs no defence.
> Thou lov'st to heare the sweete melodious sound,
> That *Phoebus* Lute (the Queen of Musique) makes:
> And I in deepe Delight am chiefly drownd
> When as himselfe to singing he betakes.
> One God is God of Both (as Poets faigne),
> One Knight loves Both, and Both in thee remaine.

The countertenor voice filled an important place in the music of the time, and the combination of lyricism and sadness in Dowland's great songs *Flow my tears*, *Sorrow stay* and *In darkness let me dwell* is ideally expressed by it. The revival of this type of song, most highly representative of that time when English composers were unsurpassed anywhere, yet without taint of the archaic about it when listened to today, is very much due to Deller's advent.

Not that, having met Dupré, he now discovered the lutenists. For years he had been working for his own satisfaction with the songs of Dowland, Campion, and others, practising them, thinking about them, but never really believing that he would have the chance to sing them in public. As a result, when he and Desmond Dupré began to perform the lutenists they did so with an already perfected art whose impact could only be irresistible. As Alfred said, "My big opportunities have come to me relatively late in life, because of my late start as a professional, and Peggy has sometimes said, understandably, "If only it could all have happened ten years earlier." But none of it *could* have happened before it did. If it had, I would not have been ready and I wouldn't have known exactly what I wanted to do with, for instance, the songs of Purcell or Dowland. As I look back over my life I trace with astonishment the logical pattern of progress it has followed, with every significant coming together of persons or events occurring at precisely the right moment. I sensed when I was a boy that this would be so, and although I've had my moments of doubt, and thought that things were not going to work out any further, they always have.

'As I say, I quite literally didn't have to stop and think what I wanted to do with these songs when my chance to sing them came; I already knew. Now, I had come to singing absolutely as a natural thing, as an instinctive thing, and ever since I had been left very much to my own devices. As a result, my interpretations are entirely the product of my own instinct and thought, and I've been rebuked by certain critics and musicologists over the years for taking liberties with rhythms and notes and being too individual in my phrasing—these are the "Dellerisms" they talk about. But I must say that, having read more deeply in recent years about the music of those earlier centuries, I am satisfied that what instinct told me to do was right, and made me approach the songs in precisely the way their composers approached them.

'I can quote three interesting authorities who bear this out. Frescobaldi, writing in the preface to his Toccatas, almost half a century before Purcell's birth, speaks of, "Time taken now slowly, now swiftly, and even held in the air, according to the expression of the music, or the sense of the words." Then there's that interesting writer Thomas Mace, who published *Music's Monument* in 1676 and said, "When we come to be masters, so that we can command all manner of time at our own pleasure; we then take liberty . . . to break time; sometimes faster, and sometimes slower, as we perceive the nature of the thing required." And finally there is John Playford the elder, in his *Introduction to the Skill of Musick*, 1654: "I call that the noble manner of singing, which is used without tying a man's self to the ordinary manner of time, making many times the value of the notes less by half, and sometimes more, according to the conceit of the words."

'I agree that one can spoil a song by bending its rhythm *too much*. I think that rhythm is of the first importance in singing, whether the song is a miniature piece lasting a minute or an aria lasting eight minutes. Every song has a basic, underlying rhythm which I call its ground swell, and one must be conscious of this from the first note to the last. One has to carry this ground swell in the mind and relate every variation of rhythm and tempo to it. And the key to defining the ground swell is, in my opinion, the text of the song: the poetry of the words.

'Both in Dowland and in Purcell the setting of the English language is perfect. In a Purcell song of the perfection of *Music for a while* it is impossible, I think, to sense which was composed first, the music or the words. They are wedded so perfectly, so subtly, that one can't believe that any other note could be possible for that particular word or syllable. This is also true of Dowland. One could look through the entire litera-ture of Dowland and not find any instance of false emphasis, a strong beat on a weak syllable. Not all the lutenist composers could do that, but their composition reflects an age in which music and words were required to serve and enhance one another. The countertenor was the most important voice in the Golden Age, and the three together made what was regarded as the perfect trinity.

'I have been told by people that because this fusion in such songs *is* perfect, the singer's only function is to sing them at a given or accepted tempo, sticking strictly to what the composer set down, and the result must be a perfect interpretation. My feeling, and absolute conviction, is that you cannot possibly take such a song as Purcell's *Sweeter than roses*, or any other great rhapsodic song, just sing the notes, at whatever tempo, and do justice to it. The whole mood of the words is what must predominate, and my approach is entirely through my feeling, my emotional feeling, for those words.

'One must make the words live in a way personal to oneself, and the rhythms get changed instinctively.

'The same applies to ornamentation. The whole purpose of ornamentation is to heighten the emotive quality of the text. But if you have to work away at a cadenza, with everything coming to a stop while you take a great breath and launch off on a clever display, it becomes unnatural and defeats its end. If you are singing *'Tis nature's voice*—'Tis nature's voice, through all the *moving* woods . . .—and you have ornamentation, or coloratura, on the word "moving", then you must move the voice quickly through it in such a way that you get the feeling of vitality. That is the whole purpose.

'It is recorded that Purcell, when composing one of his odes, could hear a chorister being rehearsed in one of his songs in another room. The singing master kept stopping the boy and trying to make him sing the ornaments exactly as Purcell had put them down on paper. Purcell called out, "Leave the boy alone. He will ornament by nature better than you or I can tell him." This is my whole approach to rhythm. If what I am singing sounds to the listener as being something which is produced, as it were, out of the air, for him, for this moment, then I have succeeded completely in what I meant to do.'

Inevitably, this emotive, instinctive approach, which, coupled with the unique quality of his voice, made Deller so distinctive and distinguished an artist, was what most offended his more pedantic hearers. Another 'Dellerism' with which he was charged was his practice of making a slight crescendo on the voice to an upper note, then thinning out the sound to piano or pianissimo. At best, it could be hauntingly successful; at worst, an obtrusive mannerism.

Deller was well aware 'that I have this mannerism, which some people feel is affected. I can only say that it isn't. Once again, it is a product of instinct arising from the mood of what I am singing as inspired by the words. I do it to heighten the poetic meaning of a particular phrase, not to produce what I think is a pretty sound. The fact that my voice is higher than most other males' is of no importance to me. Again, I know that some people object to some occasional facial expressions when I sing, and to my tendency to gesticulate slightly with my hands and sometimes beat the time. One friend says he would prefer it if I sang from behind a screen. I can only repeat that everything I do comes quite naturally, and springs more from the music than from me. My mind is not on such external things as facial expression and gestures, and I don't see why I should take any steps to control these minor foibles (though I would check them in a student). Standing absolutely still all the time is for me unnatural.*

'What matters is the ability to reach my listeners through the medium of the voice I have been given and the songs I sing with it: trying to convey to you something that is felt within me. I am not Alfred Deller, singer, performing a song; but Alfred Deller being used, if you like, to communicate with the listener on a very different plane from anything to do with technique.'

If the last remark comes periously close to sounding like the grossest affectation of them all, anyone who has been close to Deller professionally or privately can supply reassurance. To go to the other extreme, it would be fanciful to portray him as a man possessed; an ancient soul reincarnated from the age whose music he so perfectly understood and projected, entranced beyond awareness of what he was about. Yet, that

---

*He often remained seated to sing. He felt it eased formality and it also kept him on the same physical plane as his seated accompanist.

strong mystical instinct which underlay his life perhaps owed its existence to something more than his religious experiences. A less sincere, more self-conscious man might, indeed, find it convenient to persuade himself and other people that he is living proof of reincarnation. Alfred claimed nothing of the sort, invented no memories, subjective or atavistic, did not deliberately surround himself with the trappings of the times with which he was so identified: the romantically beautiful old house in which he lived was, one feels, a happy accident, rather than a chosen setting; the beard which so enhanced his 'period' appearance was grown for a specific purpose* and retained because it was more obviously right for his face than the moustache which preceded it (and, subconsciously no doubt, as a permanent deterrent to questions of masculinity). Yet, having known him, it is sometimes hard to shake away a suspicion that only his body belonged to the family into which he was born; that for all his bonhomie, warm good-will towards mankind and down-to-earth Christianity, his soul was something remote and untouchable, a spirit caught in flesh as Ariel was imprisoned in the tree—only to more purpose. His humour, great as it was, seemed to be the bright edge round a cloud of that pervading, dominant melancholy which haunts Elizabethan and Jacobean poetry, music and thought. Out of company, he was ready prey to depression and brooding despair, as he readily admitted:

'When I wake in the morning is my most vulnerable time. The longer I lie in bed, the worse my depression becomes, and it always works round to the same things: personal failure in relationships, unworthiness, the dread thought of having to retire or give up working for any other reason, the terrible idea of dying, the awful prospect of infinity. This may seem at odds with my religious convictions, but it's something I can't help

*See p. 142

and which, at times, seems capable of overwhelming me completely.'

His depressions—rarer, or less apparent, than his bursts of gaiety—were familiar to all who have been closest to him. His dark vein of melancholy, as much as his poetic sensibility, brought him into immediate sympathy with the Elizabethans. There was something in it of their morbidity: the skull, poisoned and masked like a lady, in *The Revenger's Tragedy*; Mary Stuart's dainty watch in the form of a *memento mori*; Cecil's tomb at Hatfield, with its sculpted decomposing corpse; the block and axe on Tower Hill, ever in the minds of Tudor nobles, and the gibbet and pestilence looming over the common folk. It haunted their poetry and their music: *In darkness let me dwell*; *Flow not so fast, sad fountains*; *Woeful heart with grief oppressed*; *Flow flow, my tears*... Dowland and the lutenists gave them their highest expression, and they form the most personally identified portion of Alfred Deller's repertoire.

'Reincarnation? Mystical basis? I prefer the expression "cheating time". Just occasionally—and the occasions are rare enough to remember—one achieves so perfect an involvement with the music, the words, the mood, the message, if you like, of what is being sung, and with one's hearers themselves, that there comes a feeling of complete identification and the end of personality and the meaning of time. One is outside time, out in eternity, where a gap of mere centuries is so meaningless that it ceases to exist, and so is bridged. This is the most intense, most marvellous experience I or any other artist can undergo.'

NINE

In retrieving the long-lost glories of Purcell, in communicating the Elizabethan art song in a way in which it has not been heard since the days of its origin, if then, and in touching with fresh magic the works of Bach, Handel and other composers of the Baroque period, Alfred Deller did not fail to keep in touch with earthier musical forms. His recorded repertoire includes many examples of British folk song, and, once more, his rare voice type is able to reveal qualities which have gone unappreciated in more standard performances. Though his sound is unmistakably masculine, and his approach to all that he sings is manly, that ability to convey intense emotion without sense of sexual stress which makes his voice so priceless a gift to Tudor song is a boon to folk song. There is in his renderings of such songs as *Blow away the morning dew*, *Strawberry Fair* or *Greensleeves* none of that coy, olde Englishe quaintness of so many renderings. The frank, inoffensive bawdry which still lingers in the words of many folk songs, despite the bowdlerizations of collectors, sounds self-conscious on the lips of most men and quite out of place on a woman's. Deller could sing, if he chose—and sometimes he did choose—the most outrageous of early tavern songs without offence, his sense of period making them sound as natural and unremarkable to modern ears as they were to contemporary ones. The tragedy and starkness of 'Merrie England' are conveyed vividly to us in his interpretation of such a ballad as *Lord Randall*, *The Lover's Ghost* or *King Henry* without recourse to violence of tone or exaggerated expression. That other-worldly quality of his voice puts such things into a perspective we have not before seen. It is not a case of playing Beethoven on the harmonica, or Bartók on the tubular bells. Historically Alfred Deller was re-creating, not originating. He brought back something once familiar, novel only because of long absence.

He said of this, 'Many of the folk songs are as old as, or older than, the art songs, the lute songs, of the Elizabethans, and the more lyrical examples, such as *Waly Waly*, I've always felt one must treat in exactly the same way as one would treat the art songs. They're often beautiful melodies with very touching words, the product of natural art. The countertenor voice is no more necessarily connected with folk song than is any other one type of voice, but again there is the historical fact that the countertenor was widely used when those songs were being most sung, and it is particularly suited to expressing those elements of pathos and poignancy which one finds is so many of them.'

Naturally, the sense of period which had drawn him so straight and surely to the lute songs before he could see any chance of performing them attracted him also to the even richer field of the madrigal. Here, he found a distinct function for the countertenor.

'As a preface to his *Psalmes, Sonets, & Songs of Sadnes and Pietie*, in 1588, William Byrd wrote, "If thou delight in music of great compass here are divers songs which being originally made for instruments to express the harmony and one voice to pronounce the ditty are now framed in all parts for voices to sing the same." This reference to great compass is interesting, for a large part of all madrigal literature involves the employment of two countertenor voices, often required to span close upon two octaves. This has posed a problem for the modern editor, and is usually solved by the redistribution of the parts—that is, when a part would seem to be too high for the tenor it is given to the alto, and when too low for the alto, to the tenor. This is a practical solution, since the important thing is to have these masterpieces performed, even if counter-tenors are not available. Still, it is preferable to have at least one countertenor.'

It was Deller's concern to give the madrigal its ideal expression that led him into a course of action for which the world may thank him.

Soon after he had begun broadcasting for the B.B.C., sometimes performing ensemble works with other singers who were also soloists in their own right, he realized that what was needed ideally was a group of singers accustomed to working together *as* an ensemble: people with a sense of an especial style, and with the desired mental approach, who could subjugate individuality to the work in hand.

'This arose from one or two miserable experiences,' he recalled. 'There were four or five of us, singing our heads off, with no question of an agreed balance, so that what we did made no sense at all. I came to feel that, given the opportunity and the occasion, I would like to collect my own singers who could work together regularly, get to know one another intimately and become a really cohesive team. I knew that the madrigal was essentially an intimate thing, to be performed ideally in the familiar surroundings of a great house by members of a family, or friends, singing together from the part books: people who knew each other in an intimate way, and could predict one another and compromise with one another to achieve perfect harmony. Also, I saw the madrigal as a kind of little masterpiece of vocal chamber music which could be approached in the same way and with the same musical discipline as a string quartet works. I felt that it would be possible with five or six individual voices, rehearsing five or six individual strands of music in the way that a chamber music ensemble rehearses, to achieve more real intensity than could be got from a small choir, however well chosen.'

His first venture in this direction was the formation of the Amphion Ensemble, consisting of Deller, April

Cantelo, soprano, Harry Barnes, tenor, Norman Platt, baritone, Walter Bergmann, harpsichord and piano, Desmond Dupré, viola da gamba and guitar, and, usually, a violinist and perhaps a flautist. It was not a long-lived association. All of them had engagements of their own to keep, while opportunities of appearing together were rare. What they did do, though, they did successfully; and what he had learned from the experiment emboldened Deller to form his now famous Consort.

This was in 1950. To begin with it was to be an all-male group. Instinctively, he first looked amongst his colleagues in the choir stalls of St Paul's for men he already knew and liked, and whom he knew had experience of ensemble singing. He chose Maurice Bevan, a baritone with a deep interest in the music of the seventeenth century, who had joined the choir the year after him. Maurice is still a member of St Paul's choir today, and still a regular member of the Deller Consort.

The tenors he selected were Harry Barnes, from Westminster Abbey choir, and Eric Barnes (no relation), a colleague at St Paul's. The group had no name when it gave its first performance, a broadcast of Thomas Tallis's *Lamentation*. Before long it acquired two sopranos, April Cantelo and Eileen McLoughlin, and a name, the Deller Consort. 'I remember,' said Alfred, 'we gave a concert in Stratford-on-Avon for Wilfrid Mellers, and he suggested some very high-flown name like "Cantores Britannici". This didn't seem at all convincing, and I think it was in a conversation with Walter Bergmann that the idea came up of using my own name, on the theory that, as I was associated in the public's mind with music of a particular period, anyone reading that there was going to be a performance by the Deller Consort would know just what kind of thing to expect.'

The Deller Consort proved an immediate success. A number of broadcasting engagements brought it quickly to the notice of concert agents and it was soon well established on the music club circuit and on the lists of the organizers of Britain's proliferating music festivals. Its complement has seen a number of comings-and-goings, but its standards have remained constant, its reputation and Deller's moving side by side upon the heights. Whether it performs madrigals of the English and Italian schools, sacred music of thirteenth-century France, roistering tavern songs and glees from Elizabethan England, folk music, or, more rarely, works from the nineteenth and twentieth centuries, some of them specially composed for it, its qualities are unvarying. It has performed in many countries, and been acclaimed in them all as the most perfect musical combination of its kind that it is possible to conceive. Its many recordings have earned every kind of praise whenever they have appeared, and have received many international recording awards.

This year (1980) the Deller Consort celebrates its thirtieth anniversary, with its position as one of the leading vocal ensembles as secure as ever. As *La Croix*, Paris, put it after a recent triumph there: 'The years pass; the Deller Consort remains. This famous group filled the Thèatre de la Ville for five nights and continue as strong today as the day they started 30 years ago.' The press cuttings book abounds with such phrases, in a variety of languages, as: 'truly memorable', 'unforgettable', 'very highest interpretative and technical quality', 'wonderfully polished in every respect.' One comment, in the *Schwabische Zeitung*, in 1979, seems especially perceptive:

'Thus angels in heaven may sing. One could hardly imagine purer, softer and more ethereal sounds. Their soft yet clear articulation of the consonants, their sparse use of vibrato, their incredibly assured intonation, their innate artistry in allowing the different voices to blend or the parts to separate—all this led to a recital one could hardly have imagined before one had actually listened to it.'

But it is not in its standards of performance alone that the Deller Consort carries on without its great founder and figurehead. For years, Mark Deller sang with it as second countertenor to his father, and in the early 1970s took over its direction. Under his aegis it will continue to tour the United States, South America, Germany, France, Belgium, Holland, Israel, and as far afield as Japan and Australasia, taking to many places the new and invariably inspiriting experience of hearing sixteenth and seventeenth century English music for the first time, performed with the highest degree of authority and artistry. To quote *Le Soir*, Brussels: '...His son Mark takes up the torch, and the evening spent in the company of the Deller Consort reassures us; the succession is superb.'

In fact, there is no such thing as *the* Deller Consort. Like Alfred, its members have had their own careers as soloists and in other ensembles, so that the make-up of the Consort has varied from time to time. But in more than thirty years of existence it has drawn upon a limited number of artists possessing that rather rare type of temperament which can merge self-effacingly into vocal chamber music. One founder member, the baritone Maurice Bevan, remains. In addition to others already mentioned, there have been sopranos Eileen Poulter, Mary Thomas, Suzanne Green, Honor Sheppard, Sally le Sage, Christina Clarke, Jean Knibbs and Rosemary Hardy; tenors Wilfred Brown, Gerald English, Alexander Young, Robert Tear, Max Worthley, Philip Todd, John Buttrey, Neil Jenkins, Paul Elliott and Rogers Covey-Crump; and baritones Norman Platt and Christopher Keyte.

Honor Sheppard, the longest-serving soprano, says: 'I joined the Consort formally in 1961, when I was already doing a lot of solo work, and there was a period when I could have established myself as a concert singer. The fact that I stayed to work constantly with Alfred speaks for itself. I am very much drawn to the music we both loved. But, putting aside the attraction of the music and the obvious enjoyment of the travelling, these things would soon have palled if I had not admired and loved Alfred as a man. We enjoyed a very comfortable and warm friendship throughout the years. His sense of humour appealed to me, and I was often a target for it; but I loved him, and he knew it.'

Honor Sheppard's husband, Robert Elliott, head of the School of Keyboard Studies at the Royal Northern College of Music, Manchester, who has taken part in many Deller Consort recitals as harpsichordist, adds the detail that Deller's pet names for Honor were Widow Twankey and Old Prunes and Custard, an allusion to her big dark eyes and pale complexion.

If the Deller Consort has always achieved top results, it was not only because of Alfred's inspiration, but also in spite of him. Instinctive genius led him unhesitatingly to the very core of a song's musical and poetic unity. His was the approach of the poet who has been given music, as well as words, through which to express his sentiments, and in ensemble, as well as in solo work, he did not hesitate to take liberties with rhythm and tempo. It could be disconcerting to a fellow performer not privy to his tricks.

'Anybody who joins the Consort as a new member is sitting on a razor's edge for about the first year, if not longer,' a colleague declared in Deller's lifetime. 'There were times when I thought, "I'll have to give it up", because everyone else was used to anticipating Alfred's next move, and I wasn't. When you come in you have to learn a sizeable amount of music pretty suddenly, and the trouble is you don't get the rehearsal because he doesn't like rehearsing. He leaves it to the feeling of the performance. He will let all kinds of things go at rehearsal, and rely on you when the time comes to know what it's all about and respond to what he wants. It can be terrifying, but perhaps it is all to the good, in the long run. It heightens the emotional intensity, gives an air of desperation, or something, to the performance, when we suddenly feel the tongues of fire descending from Heaven like the Pentecostal experience. This is a familiar thing to us, and I think a great deal of it is due to his magnetism. We love the music as much as he does, and we all like Alfred very much indeed, so that we respond to one another when the time comes, whatever misgivings we've had before.

'I remember a concert we had to give in Bruges which we dreaded, because we had had a heavy and tiring time of recording sessions in the South of France, and an impossibly tight schedule. We had to travel by car from where we were staying into Nice at five in the morning, fly to Brussels, take a train for Bruges, and be on the platform within about an hour of arrival. We all felt half dead, and were grumbling amongst ourselves about Alfred ever having accepted the job and there having been no chance to rehearse. We went on to the platform of an ancient hall, hardly knowing what we were doing, and straight away we found ourselves singing in a most marvellous acoustic. That performance of Byrd's five-part Mass was unforgettable because we struck that acoustic, Alfred responded to it immediately, and we responded to him. Although we rely on each other so completely, we rely upon Alfred most. If he gives, we respond, even in the most unlikely programmes which seem at first to be too long and chronologically haphazard. In a mysterious way, they come off, partly, I think, due to this magnetism of Alfred's. He's very much the slave of his feelings. If he is feeling below par, he can't understand how anyone else can possibly be feeling well. The result is that we all finish up feeling below par. If we all feel terrible, but he feels good, then we draw strength from him and recover straight away.'

Another member of the Consort added, 'One of the most disconcerting things for a newcomer is that this instinct of his for rhythmic shape can result in quite a different performance from what has been rehearsed. When he sings a solo it always goes much slower than one might expect. When one of us sings a solo, and he is conducting, he almost always goes faster than one wants to go. He feels the excitement of the music, but doesn't have to manage it technically, and so he pushes us on. I sometimes feel, "For heaven's sake, stop pushing me. This is the speed I want, and I'm not going to look at you."'

To which Alfred replied, 'I know that some of my colleagues feel this very strongly, as I would under other conductors. To that extent, I admit it. But, in my own defence, I must add that in conducting I am always conscious first of all of what a singer wants in the way of time for breathing, and so on, and my demands are realistic. What I am relentless about, though, is in insisting that this strong conviction I have about the way the piece should go must be obeyed. If I seem to drive, it is in order to wring out the music in the way I want it to come. Of course, the Consort understand and expect this, though we have differed on occasions. When I conduct other ensembles or orchestras, where you might expect there to be some difficulty, I must say I've always been given the performance I wanted. If there were objections at rehearsal, I should still insist, but give my reasons for doing so. I wouldn't stalk out in a rage.'

And the Consort members responded, 'You learn from experience that there are times to stand up to him, and times to hold your counsel. He'll get his own way if you don't argue. When you do he may resent it at the time, but he'll often come round to your point of view later.'

Desmond Dupré, who accompanied Deller more than anyone, accepted his lot philosophically. 'Alfred likes to sing a song or two before the concert, just to get his vocal chords moving, but he certainly doesn't care for much in the way of rehearsal. Even when he does condescend to go through a song beforehand, it doesn't mean all that much in terms of the actual performance. If we were to rehearse Morley's *It was a lover and his lass* only five minutes before going on stage, and then were to do it as our first item, it would still come out differently from what we'd just done. Invariably, he sings it about five per cent faster in performance, and I always try to stop him, because the rehearsal speed is about as fast as it's possible to play it on the lute. All the same, I find it less difficult to accompany him than to play with people who are basically rhythmic, yet take unmusical pauses to breathe, and so on. No one I've been with has taken more liberties with rhythm than Alfred; yet I can see the purpose of, and the rightness of everything he does, and therefore I don't find him hard to accompany.'

Since Desmond Dupré's untimely death, Robert Spencer has been the lutenist most associated with the Deller Consort and Alfred Deller's most frequent partner in recitals. He recalls wryly his own initiation.

'The first time I accompanied him, in Toledo in 1972, he reluctantly went through every song with me, and I was feeling reasonably confident. Fortunately, Mark warned me that the performance might not be so predictable, but I was flabbergasted when the evening bore so little resemblance to the afternoon. At the time it was terrifying, but subsequently I came to think he was right to be so creative in concerts. He was not a musicologist, so most artistic decisions concerning performance stemmed from a desire to communicate with audiences in modern concert conditions, an aspect of performance sometimes ignored by younger early musicians.'

Not only was Alfred reluctant to rehearse; he did no voice exercises or practice. He relied entirely on his technical gifts and his instinct for the occasion. More than one of his intimates has termed this laziness, and this seems to have been borne out, in later years at any rate, by his unwillingness to go beyond a narrow repertoire of pieces which he knew best and which were certain to please and impress audiences. This became to an extent boring and embarrassing for the Consort, who had to bear with him. He conducted no

quests for long-lost music which he might so impressively have reintroduced. He did not seek out the
challenge of works which present-day composers might
have been eager to write for him, if he had urged them.
Yet his creative influence, as Norman Platt, the former
Consort member, founder and now Artistic Director
of Kent Opera, has put it, went beyond that of most
performing musicians.

'His most important contribution lay in what he did
for composers, especially those of the sixteenth and
seventeenth centuries. His insight into the work of the
lutenists and composers of the baroque period was
profound; but his work for Purcell constituted nothing
less than a revelation and a revolution. Purcell is a
performer's composer par excellence—which is to say
that while all composers suffer from bad performance,
some, like Purcell and Monteverdi, are destroyed by it.
And the trick of making Purcell come alive had been
lost during the 18th and 19th centuries. By the 1940s
there were people, including Purcell's own successors,
Benjamin Britten and Michael Tippett, who had come
to understand him. But it was Alfred who first translated
that understanding into action, and led the movement
which resurrected Purcell into his living place among
the great. It would be difficult to exaggerate his influence in this field on present-day performers, instrumentalists as well as singers.'

It was not only in musical matters that Alfred's
associates had to come to terms with him. Though not
given to the temperamental outbursts traditionally
associated with famous singers, he could be moody
and, at times, obtuse, especially on tour. One of his
recurrent worries was that his stamina might not see
him through to the end. He felt that he began a tour
with a certain store of resources which he must husband
carefully if they were to last out. Any unexpected
demands he had to face were seen as an extra drain
upon his supply, and provoked melancholy rumina-
tions.

He watched himself and his health so intently that the result was hypochondria and a tendency to see alarming portents in small discomforts, a foible shared with many others whose personal performance is their living: one world-famous singer will not even shake hands ungloved, for fear of infection. Alfred was convinced that a Deller must inevitably suffer either from a chronic back or a weak stomach, and, unable to claim the former, settled for the latter. In fact, he was right. A gall-bladder operation a few years before his death disclosed a defect which had been there from his birth. And he confided in the present authors that when his doctor diagnosed angina he added, 'There, now—you've always hoped there was something chronic, and now you know.' Alfred lived with it cheerfully for some five years more.

Generally, though, his constitution was superb, but his gastric juices certainly governed much of his life. He was neither gourmand nor gourmet, but nothing put him in a worse frame of mind than a bad meal, or, even worse, no meal at all at the appointed time. If there was to be argument over a point of performance, anyone but a complete stranger knew the futility of embarking on it just before a mealtime. Afterwards, when the juices were flowing satisfactorily, was the moment. He ate small amounts, and preferred plain food; but it had to be served promptly, or, in his view, it would do him no good at all.

Maurice Bevan, who, in the absence of any professional manager, attended for many years to the Consort's travelling arrangements, recalls the time in Germany when they found themselves at Dortmund between trains. Knowing his man of old, Maurice had carefully booked a connection which would allow them the best part of two hours for a leisurely meal. Unhappily, there proved to be no restaurant in immediate view. His expression aghast, Alfred simply put down his bags and said, 'Well, where is it?' leaving his colleagues to bustle off in every direction looking for food.

At length, Max Worthley returned with the news that just round the corner was a buffet where fresh milk could be obtained. 'Milk?' came the agonized cry. 'Milk isn't a meal!' Eventually the station restaurant, badly sited, was found. The day and Maurice Bevan's reputation were saved.

Deller ate little, if anything, before a concert, with the result that by the time it ended he wanted nothing more urgently than a strong drink and some food. This being a need common to most artists, both were usually forthcoming, though an occasional thoughtless or disorganized host allowed introductions and prolonged conversation to intrude. Then Alfred, who could be the most charming and grateful of guests, grew more and more perfunctory in his responses. He has been heard to growl, 'If there's no food on the table in ten minutes, I'm off.' He sometimes kept his word.

With many tours at home and abroad behind him, he summed up his experience of hospitality generally as: on the Continent, considerate and well managed, often in the welcome form of an arranged visit to a good restaurant immediately after the performance, with no reception to attend; in America, most generous and well-meant, but overwhelming and often more taxing than enjoyable; in Britain, too often non-existent, with concert organizers considering their obligations over when the performance ends—a state of affairs sadly familiar to many other singers, actors, speakers, and 'performers' in public, though most have experienced delightful exceptions.

One of Alfred's most memorable experiences of hospitality was in England when the Consort was engaged to give a recital in an arts festival at Chester, for a fee which was to include accommodation for the night. Alfred, whose ways with correspondence were vague and forgetful, registered nothing in his mind about the arrangements, save that he and Desmond Dupré were to be the charge of a certain host, while their

colleagues went elsewhere. When afternoon rehearsal
finished he was not surprised to be told that the car for
himself and Desmond was waiting outside, and was
only mildly staggered to find that it was an olive green
Rolls-Royce, the largest he had seen in his life. After a
drive of half-an-hour or so the uniformed chauffeur
turned the car off the road into a private drive which
wound for what appeared to be the best part of a mile
to the front door of a magnificent house. An elegant
lady—'straight out of *Vogue*' in Alfred's description—
emerged to greet them, followed by a butler who
carried off their baggage. As they entered the hall, they
noticed the magnificence of the paintings which lined
the main stairway, and it occurred to each of them that
it would be nice to own such fine copies of Gains-
borough, Velasquez, and an assortment of other
masters.

After tea in a superb drawing-room, their still-
anonymous hostess, who had officiated with supreme
charm, told them 'I'm not giving you a heavy meal
now. We'll have dinner here quietly after the concert.
Meanwhile, I'm going to be really firm with you and
tell George to take you to your rooms and run your
baths, so that you will have plenty of time to rest and
get ready. I've put Mr Dupré into the Blue Room, and
you, Mr Deller, into the Primrose.'

Alfred recalled, 'By now, both Desmond and I were
beginning to wonder quite where we were. As we got
up to follow George, a door opened and an imposing
gentleman entered with eight dogs. We had some
conversation with him, and, again, there was absolute
charm, but no clue to identity. So Desmond was taken
off to his room and I to mine, which turned out to
have a four-poster bed with primrose hangings to
match the primrose carpet and curtains. Imagine my
feelings as I went through my door and found that
George had been thorough to a fault. He'd unpacked
my bag and laid out my partially worn dress shirt,
my suit and my dirty socks. The private bathroom was

all primrose yellow, too. The entire contents of my toilet-bag had been emptied on to a shelf, squeezed-out tube of toothpaste and all. I just stood and looked, and I heard a strangulated voice behind me. It was Desmond, standing in the doorway, saying, "Alfred! Isn't it shaming?"

They discovered later that they had been staying with the Duke and Duchess of Westminster; and that the Gainsboroughs, Velasquez, and the rest, were *not* copies. *

One of Alfred's first experiences of American hospitality, again in the most select of surroundings, had a more dramatic outcome. It was at that most superior of ladies' colleges, Sweet Briar, Virginia. At a post-performance party he had his first experience of drinking Bourbon, of which he accepted several well-filled tumblers, whose contents he innocently assumed to include a good proportion of water. He was not the first to have fallen into this trap for beginners, nor the last to pass out on standing up too abruptly. The massive form fell straight into the arms of Dupré and the diminutive harpsichordist Robert Conant. With assistance, they bore it to the best bedroom in the Director of Music's house, where it lay, motionless, until morning.

Having breakfasted—'the one and only time I've had breakfast in tails'—Alfred's problem was to get back to his room in the campus inn, whose occupants were mainly parents visiting the select young ladies of Sweet Briar, without his worse-for-wear condition being observed. A borrowed raincoat covered his evening dress, a car whisked him discreetly to a side door of the inn, and he was able to feel his way up to his room, encountering no one more formidable on the way than his two more experienced colleagues, with fresh morning faces, cheerfully making their way

---

*It was on another occasion that an elderly garden party organizer, asking Alfred to contribute a group of songs, invited him to bring along 'that banjo-fellah'—Desmond Dupré.

downstairs to breakfast. It taught him a lesson about Americans which anyone does well to learn early amongst those hospitable folk.

(In fact, events superseded this anecdote. Twenty-two years later, Alfred conducted a splendid performance of Handel's *Acis and Galatea* at the Festival of Divonne, in France. Euphoria led him afterwards to drink too much, too fast, and again he passed out and was carried to bed. He slept through until morning, when he sat up to find himself in full conducting rig, minus only his shoes, which were neatly placed beside the bed. Whenever he recounted the story he added proudly that at least he had retained sufficient control of himself to take his shoes off. No one ever told him that Honor Sheppard had done it.)

His very introduction to America at the beginning of an eight-weeks' tour in 1955 remained equally vivid in his memory. The scene is the Customs shed at New York, where he and Desmond Dupré have just stepped ashore from the *Queen Mary*. As they stand respectfully beside their baggage a large, shirt-sleeved official, chewing a cigar butt, approaches leisurely and kicks one of Alfred Deller's bags.

'This your bag?'

'Yes, and this other.'

'Say, why the beard?'

'Why not?'

'In this country only barbers and guitarists wear beards.'

'Well, my friend here accompanies me on the lute, which is a sort of guitar, so perhaps that makes me eligible to wear a beard.'

(*Thoughtful silence.*)

'Oh, ya sing? What kinda songs?'

'Elizabethan, and so on.'

(*Stunned silence.*)

(*At length*) 'Well, if ya keep quiet about it, nobody need ever know.'

Alfred recalled, 'I was too astonished to think of

taking offence, or anything. As it turned out, not biting back was exactly the right reaction and the Customs man couldn't have been kinder, telling us exactly where to go in New York to hear the best music of all kinds.'

Almost everywhere it performs in the world the Deller Consort can be certain of more than average enthusiasm for its coming, and of rapt attention from its audiences. The exception again, is in Britain, ironically the cradle of the great music which Deller helped to restore to life. Michael Tippett explained: 'One has to remember that it is not only Alfred who has experienced this contrast between the reception he gets abroad and at home. Nobody who hasn't been to Germany to perform English polyphonic music, for instance, has any idea what an excitement it is to the Germans. They are musical people, it is wonderful music, and they've never heard it before. When Alfred goes there with the Consort it's an absolute knock-out. In this country there isn't the novelty. The heyday of the discovery of our own music is a little earlier, and so we've had more experience of it. In the Americas it's different again. You have that vast continent, with vast distances between the centres in which you perform. The United States university campuses are very wealthy, with an expert on baroque music on nearly every one of them and a study of baroque that is almost continuous, so that there's a tremendously receptive field. Here, there's nothing of that kind at all.'

It was an American girl student who paid Alfred the compliment he treasured above all others: his singing, she declared, left her feeling 'all clean inside'. The most unexpectedly appreciative reception he and the Consort ever experienced occurred in Australia and New Zealand, when they visited in 1964, the first vocal ensemble to do so.

'I went with all the built-in prejudices about those countries being back of beyond, cultureless, and so on; and on each and every point I was shown up to the hilt how wrong I was. We went under the auspices of Musica Viva, which was the only society throughout Australia arranging chamber concerts. In every city we played we broke Musica Viva's box-office records; and the most incredible thing to me was that two-thirds of our audiences were young people. The sort of youth you would expect to be yelling their heads off for beat groups were queueing to come into our concerts.

'In Sydney Town Hall we performed our normal sort of programme—Byrd's five-part Mass, Italian and English madrigals, French chansons—to an audience of eighteen hundred. So many were turned away that Musica Viva had to arrange a return concert for us to give when we got back from our New Zealand tour. I remember, we arrived back at Sydney's airport from New Zealand one Sunday night, dead tired, and we had just gone through with our baggage when a porter said to me, "There's a bit of a surprise for you out there." We went through the door, and there was the place packed with young people, holding an enormous banner, "Welcome Back to the Deller Consort". It was most incredible and marvellous.'

It was markedly different from the reception they had had when arriving to take part in a performance of the Monteverdi Vespers in Paris. It was to take place in the church in Les Invalides, and a Radio-Télévision Française car was to pick them up at their hotel at 9 a.m. and drive them to a studio for a 10 a.m. rehearsal. Only one member of the party was missing, Mary Thomas, the soprano, who was flying from England and had arranged to meet them at the studio.

At the appointed hour a shooting brake arrived and they piled in and were driven off. After some time they began to pass through what were obviously the outskirts of Paris, and then reached a motorway, down which they proceeded to travel at high speed. Confidently, Alfred reassured his colleagues that they would arrive at the studio at any moment, and almost at once the car began to slow down. It halted at the entrance to a forbidding-looking place surrounded by barbed wire, with armed sentries marching up and down. In his non-existent French, Alfred sought reassurance from the driver.

'Radio?'

'Zackly.'

This they interpreted to mean 'exactly', so that when they were driven inside and then ushered out of the car into a sort of guard room they were able confidently to accept Max Worthley's theory that no doubt the radio station had to be extra carefully guarded after all those Algerian troubles. The precautions seemed to be thorough indeed, to the extent of a Security-like scrutiny of their papers, during which Max wandered across to the girl receptionist to ask if their other soprano had arrived yet. Her face assumed an expression he could not quite interpret. The other officials, already apparently mystified about something, began to register obvious alarm, turning to dismay when Max mentioned a performance of the Monteverdi Vespers. The girl seized the telephone and embarked upon a series of increasingly agitated calls, leaving someone else to explain what appeared to have happened...

How that morning was spent by the party of British scientists who had been due to be picked up by a car at that same hotel, at that same time, to be driven to the Atomic Research Station at Sacly, has never been revealed.

TEN

In 1959, while he was still at St Paul's, Deller received a letter from Suffolk:

THE RED HOUSE, ALDEBURGH, SUFFOLK

18th August, 1959

My dear Alfred,

As you may know, we are planning to rebuild our Jubilee Hall here, and with any luck it should be ready for its re-opening in the Festival next year. I am planning to write a new opera for this rather grand occasion, and it looks as if the subject will be the Midsummer Night's Dream (I am keeping this quiet at the moment because journalists are curious animals, and seize on this kind of story in a way which is occasionally embarrassing). I wonder how you would react to the idea of playing Oberon in this? It is for a big cast, and each group of people has to be carefully calculated vocally. I see you and hear your voice very clearly in this part, but before I start to write it I should love to know your reactions, and perhaps you can let us know how you are placed in May and June next year. We hope to give four or five performances in the Festival, between June 11th and 26th, and we should rehearse for four or five weeks beforehand. We would also probably do some performances abroad and in London later.

Do let me know what you feel!

Yours ever
BEN

Dear Ben,

It has taken me two days to recover from the shock! After all, my only stage experience was with the Church Dramatic Society, six performances of 'Laburnam (*sic*)

Grove', and I was young then, and my mind (pardon the word) much more alert. Do you and Peter think I could do it? If so, I would consider it a privilege to make the attempt.

Yours,
ALFRED

THE RED HOUSE, ALDEBURGH, SUFFOLK

Monday

Dear Alfred,

We do *indeed* think you can do it, and more, that you will be triumphantly successful in it! You can trust Ben, I think, to write you a lovely vocal part. Your height and presence will be absolutely right (-so will your beard!) and the part will probably be a rather static one—I mean you won't be required to turn cartwheels or climb trees—and it would be wonderful to have you with us.

Ben mentioned dates didn't he? 1st night June 11th with a month's rehearsals before, the last two weeks of them in Aldeburgh probably. The Festival itself is June 11-25. There would be five performances in the Festival (with other things for you I expect) and perhaps performances in London and abroad later on.

Ben is delighted that you will do it. So am I, dear Alfred, and most grateful.

Yours ever
PETER

His correspondents were, of course, Benjamin Britten and Peter Pears, with both of whom he had been associated in concert work at various times. It was almost the best piece of unexpected news he had received in his life. He had no reason to suppose that it would lead to a deep disappointment.

The following summer he received his vocal part for *A Midsummer Night's Dream* and was delighted. He felt that Britten had perfectly linked his voice with the character of Oberon, whom he had invested with a

Prospero-like dignity. In particular, the quiet setting of *I know a bank* struck him as a masterpiece of modern lyricism. The musical rehearsals proceeded, so far as he was concerned, smoothly and happily.

The rehearsals on the tiny stage of the Jubilee Hall, Aldeburgh, left him a shade less confident. John Cranko's production seemed to Deller perfunctory, so far as his own part was concerned, though he could appreciate that Cranko had bigger things to worry about in managing capering rustics, boy fairies, a boy acrobat as Puck, and all the rest of a largish cast, in a setting of cramped woodland. Perhaps understandably, the question of 'what to do with Deller' seemed to bear fairly low priority.

For all his great gift of mimicry and his youthful interest in amateur dramatics, both as actor and producer, Alfred Deller had never wanted to dress up and act. It needs little perception to see that he would not have made much success of it. His mimicry flared up suddenly and spontaneously out of a conversation, burned brilliantly for a little while, then was just as quickly gone. He would have been incapable of the sustained, disciplined effort of acting. The suggestion which was made from time to time that he and the Consort might assume costume to heighten the period atmosphere of some of their recitals he always rejected as irrelevant and undesirable. One exception was in 1955 when he and Desmond Dupré had undertaken to take part in a re-creation of an Elizabethan musical evening arranged by the wife of Sir Herbert Read in the contemporary setting of Hovingham Hall, Yorkshire, the home of Colonel Sir William Worsley. Having agreed with some misgivings, to wear Elizabethan dress, Alfred, accompanied by Peggy, went along to a London theatrical costumier's for a fitting. When he had donned his costume the fitter produced a small beard and popped it experimentally on to his then clean-shaven chin. On the way home Peggy remarked how well the beard had suited him, and during a caravan holiday in Ireland that summer he grew his own, which remained with him ever since.

Another costume appearance was in Australia in 1965 when *The Play of Daniel* was presented in Adelaide. 'He stood like a rogue elephant,' one of his colleagues remembers. 'He looked magnificent, until he moved, and then he seemed to run amok. He lifted up the seven-branched candlestick of the Temple, which was supposed to be a very heavy piece of furniture, like a piece of cork, and thrust it at one as though he was going to push one off the stage with it.'

He appeared in costume once more, in 1971, creating the role of Death in Alan Ridout's one-act opera *The Pardoner's Tale*, commissioned by Kent Opera, and made a striking impression.

Opinions about Alfred Deller's stage presence in *The Midsummer Night's Dream* vary between extremes. Some critics found him uninspiring, some undramatic, some wooden. Some praised his singing; but too many for his comfort concentrated on his alleged short-comings as an actor. More than one professional col-league has suggested that in venturing upon a stage he at last revealed the Achilles heel which spiteful critics had so far been unable to uncover, and that they made the most of the rare opportunity. It may have been true in one or two instances, but even the fairest-minded of critics found little to say in his praise. Michael Tippett, however, found his performance perfectly satisfying: 'I thought he was extremely good, and that it didn't matter at all that he couldn't act. He seemed to me to convey a tremendously dignified feeling. I thought that Britten had wanted to put a Prospero-like character over, and turn Oberon into a much stronger character, and Alfred had, in fact, achieved this.'

Anthony Lewis says, 'I think it was an eminently successful idea to cast him, and in the limited demands made of him he was quite sufficiently effective. The production seemed to me sensitive and sympathetic, and I thought he made a suitably commanding figure.'

The printed criticisms dismayed Deller for a time; but, as usual, his depression was not long-lived. The opera itself was widely praised, and Britten himself was well pleased with his part in it.

After its brief Aldeburgh Festival run the company performed *A Midsummer Night's Dream* again successfully at the Holland Festival and began to plan their professional and private engagements round the dates fixed for the Covent Garden season at which it was to be presented to the world at large. Then, one day, Michael Tippett received what he terms an 'agonized' telephone call from Peggy. Alfred had just had word through his agents that he was not, after all, wanted at Covent Garden. The American Russell Oberlin, whose voice was more a very high tenor than a true countertenor, had been engaged in his place.

The news had bowled Deller clean over into the blackest depression of his life, Peggy told Tippett, who recalls: 'He was quite sure that this meant that the Aldeburgh people had betrayed him, that all they had said to him was false. I spoke to him and told him that I didn't think this was so; but I explained that, false or not, this was a situation which very often occurs in our profession. You can go out as fast as you go in. I said, "Everybody's in this boat; you can't expect anything else." However, I promised to try to resolve the issue for him. I think, in fact, I asked Covent Garden about it, and it turned out to be the other way round: Britten had threatened not to have anything further to do with the production because Alfred had been turned out. It was Covent Garden who wanted Oberlin, and Britten did not. He was furious that this was so, and had given his permission very reluctantly, but, for some reason or other, hadn't written to Alfred to explain. I told Alfred all this, but his depression was extreme. He thought the whole world had been cut from under his feet.'

For Deller, 'It was certainly a low spot of my life.

I think I sang in the first performance at Aldeburgh as well as I'm capable of singing; so it was depressing to receive such a panning from the critics. As to the acting, well, I went to those rehearsals with an absolutely open mind and put myself completely into the producer's hands. What he asked me to do I did to the best of my ability, though, looking back, I think that a lot of it was wrong. I'm quite sure that I would have made a better impression from the acting point of view if I'd been treated rather more majestically, with statuesque exits and entrances and less moving around on the stage. After all, I'm an enormous man for a tiny stage like the Jubilee Hall's, and trying to sweep round in that confined space, knowing how cramped you are, doesn't enable you to move with any confidence.'

Fortunately, his natural resilience, together with the reassurances of Peggy and professional colleagues, prevented any lapsing into self-pity and quickly restored his confidence in himself. There is no doubt that he would have liked to have sung Oberon at Covent Garden, and he remained certain that he would have done so with success. What the unhappy business had not done, fortunately, was to leave him with any outsize chip on his shoulder with regard to critics in general, although he always saw himself as especially vulnerable to them:

'Even critics have inbred prejudices, like the rest of us, and in some cases, I tend to think, more so. "We have piped unto you, and ye have not danced; we have mourned unto you, and ye have not lamented." There's no pleasing some of them, and it is rather depressing to know at the beginning of a performance, when I see a certain critic there, that even if I sing particularly well in a work that suits me perfectly the most I can expect is to be ignored, while the other soloists will be mentioned. If I am mentioned, it will be in a derogatory way. Now, I find myself especially vulnerable, not in any musical or artistic sense, but because of my type of voice, and it is something to which no other professional singer, to my knowledge, has been subjected. For instance, the eminent critic of one of our national daily newspapers, in writing up a performance of the Monteverdi Vespers at the Festival Hall, said something to the effect that "The soloists included the countertenor Alfred Deller. This voice can best be described as the soulmate to Mr Hoffnung's tuba." That may be funny, or it may not; but it can only be considered in the context of humour, and playing for cheap laughs. It has no value as music criticism at all, and yet it is the remark of a professional critic.

'As might be imagined, I realized long ago that I must expect an immediate reaction of shock when I began to sing to people who had never heard me before. I have trained myself not to be upset by it, and I only hope that the audience will quickly get over this natural surprise and settle down to listen to the voice as a musical instrument, and forget about me. Thank heaven, most people do. My worst moments, I'm sorry to say, have come from professional musicians in the larger orchestras when I have appeared in more orthodox concerts. After a rehearsal at Liverpool once I heard the principal of one of the woodwind sections, a first-class player who might have been expected to know better, remark loudly to a colleague, "If my mother heard me sing like that in public, she'd disown me." And at the Festival Hall one night, as I stood in the wings waiting to begin an important concert, the leader of the famous orchestra turned to the eminent conductor and said, for me to hear, "I see we have the bearded lady with us tonight". What a charming way to begin a performance!

'I know perfectly well that what is involved here is an extra-musical consideration, arising from a quite pathetic notion of what constitutes a true man. If manliness is to mean toughness and virility, I can only suggest that the Elizabethans who used my type of voice and regarded it as altogether manly were a good deal tougher and more virile than most men today. I am a great big fellow of six foot two, and over fourteen stone; I'm the father of three, I've been a representative footballer and cricketer in my day, and I was the son of a professional gymnast; and yet, because I sing in a type of voice which has scarcely been heard for one hundred and fifty years, I can expect to be regarded as something less than a true man.

'In any case, my notion of true manhood has nothing whatever to do with these attributes of so-called toughness. A true man is someone whose whole mind and emotions are informed, and constantly being informed, so that through their exercise and the interplay between his intellect and emotions his personality develops, then his tastes and discrimination. This is nothing to do with the debased image of manhood which is constantly being thrust at us today.'

Alfred's awareness that he was treading something of a lonely path upon the heights intensified an inherited feeling of being something of an outsider. 'All the Dellers have it,' says one who married into the family and remained objective. 'There's a strong streak of detachment running through them, as if they're afraid to get too close to anyone else mentally. They're like it amongst themselves and with others. I think the lack of apparent warmth of affection in the family home made them tend to withdraw into themselves; but I also wonder, and I believe some of them have wondered, whether there is not some racial mixture in the past which might help to account for it. It might explain their exceptional darkness of hair and eyes, and some of Alfred's more mystical characteristics.'

Deller agreed. 'I have always felt a bit of an outsider. Even locally, where I have been living for years, I'm always conscious of being held at arm's length by people with whom I have daily contact. I can honestly say that I try to be natural and friendly, and talk about things they want to talk about; but I never quite get through. They always seem to me to be thinking,

"This chap's an odd bod. He's not one of us." Some friends might guffaw to hear me say it, but I am basically extremely shy, added to which, I expect, I'm automatically on the defensive for prejudice, through misunderstanding, against my voice.'

Few great artists enjoy complete *rapport* with other beings, however close they may move from time to time, and Alfred was no exception. A gap which possibly would never be bridged yawned between his good intentions and his ability to fulfil them, with the result that he was sometimes referred to as 'upstage' or 'a bit of a snob'. Neither accusation was true, though it is not hard to understand them. On the one hand stood the natural mystic, who admitted to having toyed in his youth with the notion of joining a withdrawn religious order, but knew full well that he would have been seeking a dispensation and release after a few weeks; on the other, a totally dedicated artist, who would talk entrancingly and eloquently for hours about music and numerous other subjects, yet despite brave and often delightfully successful attempts to join in on less elevated planes of discussion would eventually lapse into silent half-attention and even wander quietly away.

His hard childhood and youth had left him deeply insecure, and, as Peggy says, 'Not many people really appreciate the tremendous pressures that were on him as a countertenor before the voice had become as familiar as it is now. Other countertenors will never need to fight the battle he had to become accepted.' Also, he was never a loiterer in the 'corridors of power', television and radio circles, the clubs and pubs where the 'old boy' network flourishes. He stayed removed from them, and almost certainly missed many opportunities in his home country which influential contacts would have created for him.

Michael Tippett told the present authors in the late 1960s: 'I think Alfred belongs in the tradition of religious lyricism, which is a very real tradition, and

very deep in all our own English histories. You get
a great quality from this, but you pay a price, which is
that you get detached from a lot that happens in modern
society: you go into a fortress of some kind. This may
be your strength, of course; in any case, you have to
live it out, you can't change it. But Alfred, in addition,
has been drawn into this world of Renaissance and
polyphonic music, and I've noticed, not only in him
but in many people, that it becomes increasingly
difficult for them to find its equivalent in the modern
world, so they gradually withdraw.'

We put this to Alfred, and got a vigorous reply:
'I would deny this most emphatically. Firstly, where
music itself is concerned, my interests are by no means
confined to the periods from which my repertoire is
drawn. From the days of my youth in Hastings, when
I used to attend every Friday night symphony concert,
at sixpence a time, I've enjoyed all kinds of classical
music. I love to hear the great masterpieces of sym-
phonic writing—by some composers more than others
of course—and I can come as close to modern times as
Stravinsky and Bartók, yes, and Britten and Tippett.
Where I do stop, I'm afraid, is when I reach the writers
of serial music. I have no point of contact with them.
Music and art, for me, must have a relationship with
the human condition as I understand it; and while
I can accept highly intellectual exercises in form and
counterpoint, such as Bach's, I find this modern form
a mere series of notes, unrelated to anything, least
of all to my emotions, my heart, my soul. The gap
between it and me is too great. Sticking out my neck,
perhaps, I suggest that more people who find this music
unrewarding should say so honestly. I don't think
there is anything to be gained, either by the public or
by the composer, by merely pursuing the convention
of being "with it" and supporting things which one
really finds pointless.

'In this same way, I'm appalled to find bishops and
other people who should know better going out of

their way to encourage these "beat" groups, because they think it will please the kids. I like traditional jazz in small doses, and I quite like some modern jazz; but I loathe this beat music. I think it is an abomination, like the most outlandish examples of *avant garde* serial music, and I think it is highly dangerous from a human and sociological point of view. When I look at pictures of frenzied young people being "sent" I've no doubt at all that they're being got at by that same Old Nick who's been "sending" people since time immemorial. What the beat groups are doing is making incredible amounts of money for doing the Devil's work. I'm convinced that the whole question of dopetaking and juvenile delinquency is all linked with this rotten influence.

'As to those people who defend beat music by finding interesting traces of Gregorian chant, and so forth, in it, I believe they're talking absolute rot. You can take any music and find traces of other music in it; but it is what is made of those influences, what comes out at the other end, that matters, and what comes out in this case is an abomination.

'What I feel most strongly about, though, is the use of beat music in churches, in the liturgy. I think this is an utter mistake. There may be, in spite of what I think about it, a place for the use of beat music in the evangelization of young people in youth clubs, and other such places. But we have been told that when we enter the liturgy it is of the best that we can offer—of the *best*. We surround God with what we know to be the best in music, in painting, in light, in colour; and I do not believe for one moment that the adaptation to this debased form of music is the best we can offer. I hasten to admit that we've offered a lot of base music in the past in our liturgy—Victorian music particularly; but it has been done, however mistakenly, from the right motive, and in the way of a genuine impulse. I see beat Masses, and so on, as a cheap and deliberate device for luring young people into empty churches.'

His concern for the church which had so strong an influence on his life remained deep, but he denied that he was a good Christian. 'I don't pray enough. I entertain too many doubts and fears which only get in because of weakness of faith; and I constantly tell myself that I should do more for people. I know I would never have made a monk, but I often wonder whether I might not have made a priest. I'm aware that what I have been able to do in music has given something to a lot of people. I tell myself that my work is a form of prayer, and a worth while act. Where I feel that I have failed is in not reaching the people who do not hear me sing. There are so many old and lonely people in this world, for instance. I tell myself that if I were to telephone the hospital and offer to visit them I should be doing something much more valuable. Of course, I can't, because I am always travelling or caught up in some other way, and there's very little left over outside my work; but the sense of failure is always with me. I feel that, apart from my music, I have not developed.'

He left the choir of St Paul's in the summer of 1962. He was fifty years old, an age well beyond that at which most breadwinners would risk cutting themselves off from a regular income, and at which the average singer would be looking ahead to retirement. But he had been aware for some time that he was spending less time in the choir-stall than on the concert platform, and that there existed certain resentments amongst colleagues over his constant use of deputies in his cathedral work. A gentle push from Canon Collins launched him into full-time freelancing.

He left St Paul's with much regret, perhaps sensing that he would be leaving behind more than the music of the church. His relationship with religion had owed much to emotion, had satisfied a large part of his emotional hunger. It saddened him to think that, from now on, he could expect that relationship to diminish more and more under the pressures of a career which from its beginning had owed the church so much. Still, when touring, he attended Mass whenever possible, and was a churchgoer to the last. He retained his link with St Paul's for a time as a committee member of Christian Action, under the chairmanship of Canon Collins; but he rarely managed to attend meetings. His lessened contact with the church worried him, though it should not have done. The churchmen who most influenced his life are unanimous in their opinion of the quality of his Christianity, and he was realist enough to know that he could not be other than what he was.

'To be brutally honest, I'm a one-track person, and that track is music. I can't conceive of life without it, and I would be a very depressing person to live with if it were taken away from me. No, there it is, and I am not a big enough person to change things now.'

ELEVEN

The end of his association with St Paul's freed Alfred at last to accept more of the engagements awaiting him outside Britain. He had made his first trip abroad—the first of his life for any purpose—in 1949, at the age of thirty-seven, to sing in Geneva. He had gone hesitantly. It was his first experience of flying, too, and nothing less than so important an engagement would have persuaded him off the ground. He never lost his dislike of air travel, suffering perils quite unapparent to his fellow travellers. Driving him to Heathrow airport one morning was one of the most gloom-laden experiences of our own lives: he was a different man from the effervescent guest of the previous evening. Necessity, however, dictated that he fly thousands of miles each year, leaping from country to country with sometimes barely a day's rest between taxing performances. In truth, he would have preferred not to travel anywhere, ever. He appreciated none of its forms and took no interest in the places he visited. While his colleagues saw what sights time permitted he lurked in his hotel room.

By trial and error the Deller Consort disciplined their travelling into a manageable routine. The first obstacle was Alfred's propensity for scribbling dates, information and programme details on the backs of used envelopes (a hark-back to his poems to Peggy on lino tiles?) He employed no full-time road manager, but relied on agents in various countries for travel and accommodation. Much of this burden was borne for years by the well-organized Maurice Bevan, who was relieved at length to be able to transfer it to Mark Deller.

Desmond Dupré used to relate that on their first

American tour together Alfred took an amount of baggage which could only be described as fantastic, including a suitcase full of bound music and another crammed with superfluous clothes, both of which remained unopened in their New York agent's office. Indigenous food abroad had no appeal to the all-important gastric juices, and he made no attempt to learn to speak other languages. He could interpret enough from them to aid his instinctive interpretation of foreign song, and he learnt the words phonetically. It was the music which guided him to an accurate feeling for everything he performed. He travelled, in fact, in order to do the only thing he could do and wanted to do: to get out in front of an audience and sing.

In late years this became more and more his pre-occupation. His mind, in Peggy's term, had become 'one-track'. He became restless about his audiences' behaviour and response. In those long periods of introspection he must often have brooded on the longevity of his voice and wondered how much longer he would keep it. Peggy dreaded the prospect of his eventual retirement. Teaching would have been no-where near a substitute for performing. He would not have known how to manage retirement, and no one could have helped him. He had no leisure resources, went to no concerts, theatres, films. Although he had been a notable young cricketer he would never bestir himself to travel the few miles from his home in Kent to the historic county ground at Canterbury and spend a day in the sun. He watched some cricket on television, and the tennis at Wimbledon, as well as a lot of news and current affairs programmes. Otherwise, beyond a crossword, much reading, and a little plain gardening there was little for him outside music.

Poetry was a solitary pleasure he could carry with him wherever he went. Honor Sheppard says, 'Some-times he would ask me if I had a few minutes to spare. This invariably meant that he had found some passage of poetry, or a paragraph in a book, which he found moving or stimulating and wanted to share. He knew that he had in me a very ready listener.'

His hypochondria manifested itself in rows of bottles in the bathroom cupboard, most of them natural tonics which he had sworn by for a time before discovering something he believed more effective. He smoked a pipe, and sometimes cigarettes, though never inhaling. His throat preoccupied him much less than his stomach, until, that is, immediately before he was due to sing. Then, if he could convince himself he was going to suffer a frog in the throat, he would begin clearing it over and over again until all his colleagues felt their throats going in sympathy. Audiences in the front rows often heard him before they saw him, and sometimes, to their distress, the throatclearing continued on the platform itself. Occasionally the Consort would hear a despairing groan issue from him as he surrendered to the certainty that his voice was about to seize up altogether. They exchanged knowing glances. As soon as the music started his throat would be forgotten.

Since all his tours were successful he could return home elated, though exhausted. He and Peggy would go out to a restaurant for a meal, over which he related his experiences and gradually unwound. The night's sleep was generally enough to restore his energy. After a continental-style breakfast, followed by a pipe over three or four crossword clues, he would make eagerly for his small, cluttered study where the accumulated post awaited him. Work, and the continuing prospect of work, were his greatest revivers.

Home, for the last twenty-odd years of his life, was Barton Cottage, in the village of Kennington, near Ashford, in the heart of the Weald of Kent. As they went from one place to another the Deller family had had dreams of living in the country. It was while living at Bickley, on the northern fringe of Kent, that they began to spend holidays in the Kennington district, where Barbara Headley owned an orchard containing holiday huts—ideal and cheap for Peggy and the children.

One morning the boys came in with the news that there was 'a super house' for sale in the village. 'You ought to go and see it,' they told their mother, 'you've always loved looking at houses.' So, 'for fun', she got the key.

The building itself proved to be romantically half-timbered, of the fifteenth and sixteenth centuries, set in a huge, overgrown garden, full of possibilities to the imaginative Dellers, and completely rural—there were even pigsties at the back. It was very dilapidated-looking and Peggy expected a derelict interior.

She got an agreeable surprise. The house had been completely converted from two or three cottages, and modernised throughout. Though it had been empty for three years, it was in perfect order. The only essential work that had to be done before they could move in —as, of course, they did, having fallen in love with it— was the strengthening of the foundations, which turned out to be solid oak-trees, and Saxon.

Only a few months before Alfred's death they discovered, near the duck-pond, a fine old brick well. They had it cleaned out and refurbished, and installed an electric pump for the filling of the pond, an operation which Alfred delighted to perform from the comfort of the sitting-room.

It was from this tranquil base that Alfred developed his career to its ultimate, while the hitherto nomadic family at last enjoyed a settled life. As a parent, he has been described by one of them as 'perhaps a little distant'. Peggy recalls how, earlier in their marriage, it used to irritate her to hear him praising in other people's children qualities to which he was apparently oblivious in his own. The children recognized the extent of the demands made upon his mental and physical stamina by his work and travelling, and accepted some lack of intimacy without resentment. They found ample compensation in their mother.

There were frequent family reunions which, if he didn't fully demonstrate it, Alfred enjoyed as much as anyone in his rôle of slightly aloof patriarch.

When relaxed and in the mood he shared many hilarious times with them all, especially round·the card table. Pontoon, for small stakes, was a general favourite. His Boy Scout's love of camping never quite left him. When the children were small the family would go on camping holidays to Scotland and the Norfolk Broads. Gradually, Alfred's propensity for roughing it decreased. An essential part of their camping equipment became 'a table and chair for father'. Every spring since moving to Barton Cottage he was heard to declare his intention of taking a small bivouac tent on to the Wye Downs for a few nights. He and one of the present authors talked on and off for years of going on a walking tour together. Either enterprise would have seemed increasingly ludicrous to anyone who knew Alfred Deller or Michael Hardwick; but the mystique of the open air remained potent for Alfred.

Peggy, who admits that she once begrudged him his months of travel to all parts of the world, while domestic and economic necessity kept her at home, came to terms with their lifestyle. All who know her share admiration for the way she aided and tended a man whose moods and propensities would at times have tried a saint's patience, and whose domestic ineptitude and lack of all business acumen must often have brought her near to despair. As man about the house he was totally incompetent, knew it, and had no desire to reform. Anything mechanical defeated him utterly. It was useless for Peggy to seek his help in removing an obstinate light bulb from its socket, or screwing a fitting to a wall. After a cursory glance he would declare the undertaking impossible, and wander away, leaving her to get on with it. When the problem was abstract, rather than practical, it was a different matter. He was always a willing listener to people's problems and seldom at a loss for advice to give, a manifestation of the priest *manqué* which Peggy, who saw more of it than anyone, regarded as suspect.

'It worried me at times, because people so readily accepted what he told them. He had a gift with words and a remarkable memory for anything he'd read, so that he could very easily produce a quotation which seemed to fit the case, but didn't really, if you stopped to think about it. People would go away thinking him a marvel of wisdom, an oracle of some sort; then they'd come back for more, and perhaps find that he had lost all interest. He helped a lot of people in very practical ways, but generally he couldn't keep it up, so that I was sometimes left trying to cope with their troubles where he had dropped them.'

Again and again with Alfred Deller, the same cause and effect were seen. His whole thought and energy were focussed upon his career. Little remained for externals, although, occasionally, good intentions flared up, burned briefly, then were snuffed out abruptly as the main demand reasserted itself.

All three children are now married and gone away, although Mark lives just down the road, at Wye, his career now entirely devoted to directing, managing and singing with the Deller Consort, directing the Deller Academy and Stour Music, and guest-conducting choirs in many countries where the name of Deller is is revered. His career brought deep gratification to his father, who once admitted to us that he had scarcely allowed himself to hope that his son would share his experience of making the transition from promising boy singer to adult professional, least of all as a countertenor.

'When Mark went into The King's School, Canterbury, at fourteen, I thought that would be the moment for it all to end, which would have been natural enough. Instead, he identified himself with the school's music straight away, especially with the re-formed Madrigal Society, and, what's more, as an alto, though I had done nothing to push him into trying to sing across the break as I had done. In due course he wrote to tell us that he was going to try to get into Cambridge University as a choral scholar. He came and stayed overnight with us on his way to take his voice test. I asked him what the test piece was to be. He had chosen *Return, O God of hosts* from *Samson*. I sat down at the piano and said, 'All right, I might as well hear it.' He sang it through, and I remember making one or two observations, such as 'I wouldn't breathe there' and so on. That was all the coaching he ever had from me before taking that test and coming first out of more than twenty candidates.'

After three years at Cambridge Mark became a lay clerk in Salisbury Cathedral and taught for some time in the choir school, working as his father had done on a farm, to augment his income. Also following his father's example of marrying the boss's daughter he married Sheelagh Benson, the daughter of his headmaster there. His interest in organizing concerts and musical groups at Canterbury, Cambridge and Salisbury, where he was Artistic Director of the city's first Festival of the Arts in 1966, prepared him well to assume the direction of the various enterprises associated with the Deller name. Mark and Sheelagh have three sons, the eldest named Thomas after his great-grandfather, the Sergeant, and Alfred after his grandfather.

Mark Deller resembles his father in voice, although it is smaller and paler, less ripe than Alfred's. It is his younger brother Simon who has inherited the physical characteristics of massivity and facial resemblance. He sings bass. His voice broke exceptionally early, forcing him to leave Canterbury Choir School. He did well academically at the City of London School, where he managed to keep up his interest in music, which he studied as first subject when he went on to Nottingham Teacher's Training College. He married a fellow student, Mollie Stallard, and is now a lay clerk at Guildford Cathedral, Surrey, and deputy headmaster of the preparatory school which provides the cathedral's choir-boys. There are two sons, both members of the choir.

The other child, Jane, in whose pretty face the dark Deller eyes appear most strikingly of all, qualified as a teacher before marrying John Jackets, an agronomist with the Ministry of Overseas Development. His work abroad keeps her furthest from home of any of the children.

With the family scattered at last, Peggy carried calmly on, doing herself the things Alfred could not or would not do, making the arrangements he neglected, tending relationships. And when he performed in London or in Kent she was invariably there to hear him, never obtrusively as the great artist's wife, never in the front row where he could see her. She listened to him sing more than anyone did, except his Consort colleagues, and yet she admits that she is not 'musical'. A combination of her experience of his performances, and a feeling for the little movements and sounds of the audience around her, told her when he had done something not quite his best. She was far shrewder than to tell him so afterwards, but if he gave her the cue, perhaps by questioning aloud something he himself had sensed, she would gently tell him what she had thought. He always took the point.

Peggy's own creative talent is for painting. It is a skill that had lain latent for most of her life through lack of time to develop it, until, left alone with Alfred away for at least half of each year, she resumed evening classes in Ashford. There was plenty of encouragement from the Stour Valley's many professionals—John Ward, R.A., Gordon Davies, and others. She had her own exhibition in Canterbury and showed a painting in a Royal Academy Summer Exhibition.

Her work ranges from still life to landscapes, many of them realized in the stimulating artist's light and terrain of Provence. The Dellers had been drawn to the region by professional circumstances in the late

1960s, a time when ancient and neglected properties could be bought for very little. Disappointed over a two-room farm cottage which was withdrawn after a price of £200 had been agreed, they found Le Clos, a completely derelict sixteenth century farmhouse near Forcalquier. It looked ideal for the establishment of an enterprise which had been in Alfred's mind for some time, a Deller Academy, specializing in the teaching of sixteenth and seventeenth century English music.

We have said that Alfred Deller could never have substituted teaching for performing, and until the creation of the Academy he did little teaching at all. Inevitably, many young men inspired by his example applied to him over the years. He helped some of them, but his constant absences prevented anything sustained. Also, when he did teach he tended to commit himself as totally as in performance, emotions and all, and the effort drained him. He declined a flattering invitation from Sir Keith Faulkner, principal of the Royal College of Music, to join the staff to teach solely the counter-tenor voice. He served as visiting professor to the Reinische Schule für alte Musik, at Cologne, which involved only brief visits. In 1968, for the spring semester, he was the first musician to be honoured with the Bingham Chair of Humanities at the University of Kentucky. And in his last years he was visiting professor of early music at the Royal Northern College of Music, Manchester. For the most part, though, those who wished to learn from him had to do so by hearing him perform, either in person or through the media of radio and recordings.

Although his career owed much to radio, from the very start of the B.B.C. Third Programme, he was by no means a frequent broadcaster; again, no doubt, largely due to that refusal to ingratiate himself with the musical hierarchy. As the discography shows, however, he made a great many recordings, mostly of a technical excellence worthy of his art which is represented in all its facets and range of repertoire.

After making his first 78 r.p.m. discs for H.M.V. he was approached by the Dutch harpsichordist Gustav Leonhardt, then teaching at the Vienna Conservatoire, who had been asked by the Vanguard Recording Society Inc. of New York to make recordings of Bach cantatas and Elizabethan and Jacobean music with a vocal ensemble. Would Deller care to take part in these recordings? He would be delighted; and Vanguard, delighted with the results, offered him an exclusive contract. H.M.V. released him, with the consequence that almost all his own and the Consort's considerable recording activity for more than a decade was under the aegis of Vanguard's Bach Guild label. These superb recordings brought him into association with many of the world's leading instrumental ensembles specializing in his periods of music and made him familiar to American and European music-lovers. Because Vanguard recordings were not at first distributed in Great Britain, his exclusive contract with the company kept him for many years little appreciated here. In 1966, however, he terminated the Vanguard contract in order to join Bernard Coutaz, of the French Harmonia Mundi recording company, in founding Alfred Deller Recordings, for which he and the Consort recorded almost exclusively. Their recordings have world-wide distribution through Harmonia Mundi, and have been acclaimed wherever they have been heard, including countries where Deller never appeared in person and the music of Purcell, Dowland and Campion has hitherto been unknown.

Like many artists, Deller enjoyed a love-hate relationship with recording. He disliked the tyranny of technical demands and the financial necessity of getting through the maximum amount of work in the minimum time. He refused to indulge in the modern practice of assembling a clinically perfect performance by constant retaking and editing-in of passages which have not been one hundred per cent; though he would edit where a distinct flaw was noticeable. He would not subscribe to the other extreme, what he described as 'Let's all be jolly together—hit or miss, so long as we get the spirit of the thing'. This he regarded as the amateur approach. He disliked the inescapable long periods of waiting about in the recording studio, listening to other artists doing their part and then having to get up 'cold' to the microphone to do his. Constant stops for technical reasons and to listen to playbacks destroyed the continuity of the work for him. Experience, however, taught him to overcome these inhibitions and to feel in the recording studio that he was singing before a perfectly mannered and warmly responsive concert audience.

Again, like many colleagues, he was critical of his early recordings; not of the quality of his and the Consort's performances, but of what he saw as a certain inhibition of style, for which he was inclined to blame the technical side of things.

'I realize when I play one of those early recordings how much faster and more assured we are today in performing, say, English madrigals. Everything is there, but too carefully done. With my lack of experience at the time, I must have let my natural instinct for tempo be moderated by what I thought was the vital necessity to have every part heard distinctly. So everything was taken a little stodgily, whereas today we perform those same works quite differently and much quicker, and yet without losing a thing.'

For all his reservations, he was conscious of his great debt to recording and to the mysteriously gifted technicians who joined their skill with his to produce the discs which have multiplied his world audience countless times over.

Almost all his Harmonia Mundi recording was done in the tiny church of All Saints, Boughton Aluph, which has stood since the thirteenth century in the rural peace of the Stour Valley, only a few miles from the urban sprawl of Ashford. Alfred first became aware of the remarkable acoustical properties of the remote church, when John Ward, who also lives nearby, persuaded him to have a look at the superbly proportioned workmanship of the interior. Alfred did more than look: he sang a few bars. The acoustic astonished him.

The Harmonia Mundi engineers came from France, to stay a few days at a time in Barton Cottage and record in the church, under the artistic direction of Bernard Coutaz. They worked fast, in accordance with Alfred's dislike of hanging about; perhaps two days to make a complete album. He listened to the results just once, in complete isolation. He would not go back and re-take and did not fuss over the mixing. He believed that too much hearing of a piece or a passage destroyed the critical faculty.

He was still recording only weeks before his death. Almost aptly, his last issue was a selection of Purcell songs accompanied by Wieland Kuijken, bass viol, William Christie, harpsichord, and Roderick Skeaping, violin. It takes its title from one of them, *Music for a While*, the song which had come virtually to be regarded as Alfred Deller's 'signature-tune'. There are no unissued Deller recordings for us to anticipate, but coming years will see many reissues and freshly grouped selections. We have been deprived of a number of projected recordings, notably a re-make of the big Purcell *Ode for St Cecilia's Day*. However, more than one hundred and thirty issues, more than half of them currently available, make a rich field for the collector, and the Deller recording tradition will continue through the Consort.

TWELVE

The ancient house in Haute Provence, Le Clos, never did become the premises for the Deller Academy. The conversion needed was too extensive and costly. It could only be done piecemeal, with the usual difficulties accompanying a building project in a foreign land, supervised by intermediaries. It was never more than half completed in Alfred Deller's lifetime and was used only as a holiday retreat and a base for running the Academy, which in 1971 came into being in modified form, first at the Abbaye de Senanque, then after three years, at Lacoste, some forty miles from Forcalquier.

It began with three professors, Alfred, Desmond Dupré and Walter Bergmann, lasting two separate weeks, with twenty-five students attending each. At Lacoste, since 1974, it has occupied ten days' consecutive study of voice, harpsichord, recorders, viols and lutes, based entirely on the English music of the sixteenth and seventeenth centuries, especially the lute song repertoire and the music of Purcell. Some seventy students attend lectures and demonstrations by five professors and visiting specialists in the respective subjects. They come from all parts of the world. As many as half each year are making a return visit, and two have attended every year since inception. Much though Alfred Deller is missed, both by students and teachers, demand for places continues as keen as ever, with more applications than can be accepted.

The setting is fantastic, the music superb, the company what Alfred would have termed a 'conspiracy of of spacious song'. The students are lodged locally and there are activities every day from nine a.m. until midnight, with a concert every evening in the local church.

This and his own example of creative performance are two of Alfred Deller's major legacies to the renaissance of early English music. Their continuance is assured; and so, one hopes, is that of another, the international festival, Stour Music, held each year in Alfred's part of Kent.

It was conceived something like a year after his first visit to Boughton Aluph church with John Ward. Over tea in the front porch of Barton Cottage Alfred suddenly remarked 'Wouldn't it be wonderful if we could have some music in that church?'

A committee of local enthusiasts was formed and the first Stour Music took place in 1963. It lasted one day, and it was not in Boughton Aluph church. In the morning there was a talk on early instruments in the parish church of the picturebook village of Chilham, down the road to Canterbury. That afternoon Alfred and the Consort appeared as soloists in a Bach concert there with the Philomusica Orchestra and a choir drawn from many parts of the country, the items including the Magnificat in D. In the evening there was a concert in the evocatively atmospheric setting of the small, white-pillared hall of Olantigh, the stately Stour Valley home of Mr William and Lady Prudence Loudon. The following year the festival lasted three days, and Boughton Aluph church was used for the first of many times. The Olantigh concert was sold out, and was to be at every Stour Music since, until it became no longer available in 1976.

It is impossible to conceive any more satisfying musical occasion than, for example, a performance at Olantigh of a Purcell work by the Deller Consort and the contemporary instruments of the Concentus Musicus of Vienna, with a *cordon bleu* buffet in the interval and an informal mingling of artists and audience over drinks in the Old Brewhouse afterwards. Stour Music has always reflected that principle of Glyndebourne's founder, the late John Christie, to offer 'Not the best we can do, but the best that can be done anywhere.'

The festival developed and spread with each succeeding year, embracing churches and other venues for
concerts, recitals, talks and exhibitions of art. A con-
trasting attraction, which the present authors had the
pleasure of devising and directing for several consecutive years, was a final evening of words and music
at Olantigh with leading actors and actresses appearing
with the Deller Consort and other musicians. Donald
Sinden, Janet Suzman, Barbara Jefford, Richard Pasco
and Barbara Leigh-Hunt are representative of the guest
artists of these packed occasions when the lutes and
viols and baroque sentiments gave way to laughter and
a general sense of unwinding. There were also some
notable 'one-man' shows by such scintillating individualists as Paul Jennings and the late Joyce Grenfell.

Alfred regarded Stour Music as the high-spot of his
year. Fortunately for its survival—and it will go on
without him, now lasting an entire week—it was not
handled entirely by him, but by a committee, fired by
his enthusiasm, with Mark as artistic director. It was
Alfred's enthusiasm that coloured the occasion, and
their respect for him that persuaded distinguished
artists to travel from abroad to perform for small fees
and consider it a privilege to do so.

The heroine of the entire venture, though, is Peggy.
Throughout the festival period, and well before and
after it, her life and home are completely disrupted.
Barton Cottage is turned into an hotel for visiting
artists and an open house for patrons. A large marquee
in the garden houses a running buffet and bar, conducted
by Peggy and devoted non-professional helpers who
stream across the croquet-lawn carrying replenish-
ments one way and used crockery, cutlery and glasses
the other. The sun generally shines in the last week in
June when the festival is held—'Stour Weather', they
call it; English, French and German voices inter-
mingle, as do tail coats and sports shirts.

The marquee empties suddenly, as slightly tense
musicians and audience move to the fleet of cars which

will ferry them to Wye or Boughton Aluph. Those who are not performing or attending lounge on in deck-chairs, contemplate the ducks on the little pond, learn lines for the evening show. Chatter and washing-up sounds drift from the kitchen.

Then the tea things begin to appear. The trestle tables are laid again; and back come the afternoon's performers, happy and relaxed now, full of banter about the way the concert went, the little things the audience didn't notice, the in-jokes, and the reminders to Peggy, who needs no reminding, that they must be got to a certain train in order to catch their flight at Heathrow.

And amongst them, pausing to smile over a story someone is telling here, to nod agreement to a musical assertion there, moves the benign shade of Alfred Deller, rejoicing quietly at this manifestation of what he set out to achieve. It will be more at Stour Music than in any of the world's concert halls that we shall feel the brush of his presence, before he wanders away to seek his solitude again.

The knowledge that he had angina made no difference to his career. His doctor rightly supposed that he was glad to know the truth and could settle down to live with it.

He put no limitation on the number of engagements. He travelled as widely as ever, and continued to sing and conduct. Now that Mark was in full charge of the Consort he could almost always be with his father and, without trying to cosset him, lessen in many small ways the strains. One instance was the increasing number of duos the two of them performed, reducing Alfred's burden of solo work.

It was immediately before a concert began—that moment when tension is always greatest—that he began to feel ill effects. Sometimes, in his last year or so, he would have to take an unscheduled break for some minutes in mid-programme. While conducting a performance of Orazio Vecchi's madrigal opera

L'Amfiparnaso at the Festival of Divonne, France, in June, 1979, he had to leave the stage for half an hour before he could continue. The same happened during a repeat performance at La Rochelle, five days later.

Two days after that, July 4, he had worked all day at a television recording in the South of France, and had just got back to his hotel, when he suffered an exceptionally bad bout, which Mark suspects may have been a heart attack. By next morning, though, he was feeling perfectly well and was back at work.

Ten days later he was in Bologna, a rare visit to Italy whose heritage of ancient music, calling for delicate singing and meticulous ensemble, has been so eclipsed by the pyrotechnical demonstrations of blustering tenors and coloratura sopranos. Alfred and the Consort sang much Italian music of the highest order —Monteverdi, Marenzio, Gesualdo—wherever they went, but almost never in Italy itself.

He was there this time not to perform, but to sit on the select jury of an international singing competition. On the Thursday afternoon he had so severe an attack that hospital admission and intensive care were necessary. He asked them to telephone Mark, in England, but to ensure that Peggy was not told. Mark didn't hesitate to ignore this. By next afternoon he and Peggy were at Alfred's beside. He was insisting that he was all right, angry not to be allowed to get up. It seemed that he would make a good recovery. But at eight o'clock the following Monday morning, July 16, he died peacefully.

The news reached Britain startlingly by its unexpectedness. In his tribute in the quarterly journal *Early Music* Sir Michael Tippett wrote: 'I judge my last sight of him to have been a true meeting. (He would have understood it so.) I looked in at the B.B.C. News and there he was in close-up. The head had no body; the mouth seemed over-large in the face, because wide open: singing so close to me that the subtlest muscular movements were visible. He sang the opening bars of Purcell's *Music for a while*. A poignant emotion, indeed, to be comforted in the moment of grief by the man himself, though already passed out of life. The voice had as always its own inviolable purity. It sounded so gentle, so alone, as almost to be frail (a trick, I think, of the machine). But a frailty, certainly a purity (when set against concert and operatic spectaculars) that is also a strength; some quintessence, surely, of our great and mutual art.'

He was brought home to Kent. After a service at the parish church of Kennington, a little way down the road from Barton Cottage, he was buried in the ancient churchyard of All Saints, Boughton Aluph, beneath an ash tree on the North side, at a point where his voice had reached countless times during concerts and recording sessions. It was a gorgeous day. The Stour Valley was radiant.*

In preparing this ending to Alfred Deller's life story, we put it to Peggy and Mark that if his conviction were correct that he had been in some way singled out by God for his purpose, and his destiny shaped accordingly, the circumstances of his dying must conform to the pattern. They agreed readily that it had. In many small ways, some no doubt circumstantial, he seemed almost to have been served notice that his mission was fulfilled.

In January 1979, after years of fruitless pleas from Peggy, he at last cleared out his files and sorted his papers. It was a major operation, but it left his affairs in some semblance of order. In March, instead of waiting until the normal autumn sessions, he went to France to make what was to be his last record, choosing Purcell songs, many of which he had not sung for years. His last words on the disc are '...that makes me wish to die.'

In June, shortly before Stour Music was due, Peggy

---

*One aim of the Alfred Deller Memorial Trust is to restore and reopen the large south-transept window of Boughton Aluph Church.

had a fall in the house and fractured a femur. (Being Peggy, she lay on the floor all night, rather than wake and upset Alfred.) Clearly, she would be in hospital throughout the festival and for some time afterwards. Her usual volunteers would cope with the practicalities of catering and travel arrangements for the visiting performers; but something impelled Peggy to want to hear Alfred sing in Boughton Aluph church. Again, he had chosen some Purcell songs he had long neglected.

The hospital doctors were doubtful about letting her out for that Wednesday evening. Her injury was not far enough advanced in healing. She persisted and they agreed to bend the rules. Her physiotherapist took her in her own car and she heard the concert from a wheelchair. It was the last time Alfred ever sang in England, and she was there.

The shock of his death, so soon after this, was ameliorated by the relief that he had never had to suffer the decline and loss of his voice. The fear of boredom and decay was never realised. He died working, his reputation untarnished and admiration for him undiminished. He had often given thanks for apparently being 'God's darling'. The conviction seemed to have been finally justified.

When Peggy got back to England from Bologna she found a letter awaiting her. Alfred had written it to her on arriving in Italy, and it had been in the post when he died. It is so characteristic of him in many ways that Peggy gives us kind permission to print it here, in its entirety.

10th July 1979.
Royal Hotel Carlton
Bologna.

Dearest Peg,

What a lark it all is, chalk it up to experience they say. To begin at the beginning, checked in at Heathrow in good time, the British Airways girl said 'Shall I book your bag through to Bologna?' upon which I naturally said 'Yes please': everything on time in Paris, but, by the way, the journey from Charles de Gaulle to Orly West took 50 minutes by bus. I then had to check-in (having walked up two floors and a considerable distance) finally made it with 30 minutes left of my available two hours. Upon arrival at Bologna I was met as promised by nice English-speaking young man—but of my bag no sign; the French had impounded it at C. de G. There followed 40 minutes' form-filling, and hopefully the bag should arrive here tomorrow a.m. It seems that unless baggage is collected in Paris the French Customs hang on to it. I remember (too late) that this is the normal (abnormal) French practice. So arrived here—by the way, the v. best hotel in Bologna, 'nothing else good enough for you, Maestro', said the young man, which is one more indication that my fee is not large enough —around 3 p.m. yesterday with but the clothes I stand up in—and lie down in, as a matter of fact. The hotel is the Italian equivalent of Divonne without the advantage of a garden, but as the temperature is in the 80's, bright sunshine, and my velvet jacket etc. is somewhat ludicrous, I stay in the air-conditioned hotel (my first session this evening) and play up that eccentricity of character implicit in 'mad dogs and Englishmen.'

By the way, talking of eccentricity, when I first used the bathroom upon arrival I saw one of those sachet-things which I took for a face-freshener, opened it up and gave my face a thorough going-over, only to discover that it was intended for cleaning shoes!! After about 30 seconds the glue-like substance started to gum-up my eye-lids and the whole face became somewhat 'congealed'; hot water, soap and scrub like crazy.

Of course all this inconvenience is somewhat nullified by the knowledge of my 'carte blanche', I just write my room number and signature on all the bills, drinks, meals, etc., but it does not endear me to the mode of life—like being confined in a luxury prison. The Harnoncourts are not here, Concentus Musicus in South America, and it seems that I shall be the only non-Italian on the Jury, so will have to resort to the old thumbs-up or thumbs-down to indicate my decision—but age-old Italian tradition for that. Didn't the Caesars resort to it during the Christian persecutions?

A Singularity of Voice

Hope you are still managing the stairs successfully,
Molto, molto amore,
Alfred.

THIRTEEN
A CONVERSATION
WITH DELLER

Alfred Deller's was so personal an art, and he expressed his views upon it so fluently in conversation, that we feel that the reader might care to have, in his own words, the answers to certain questions we put to him.

Picture him, one morning, in the heavily beamed drawing-room of Barton Cottage. A small log fire smokes idly in the vastness of the inglenook fireplace, contributing only atmosphere to the electrically heated room. Beside it, Alfred inhabits his tall winged chair, his back to the window, the bearded face dark-shaded from the light. He wears a flame-coloured woollen cardigan of uncertain age which Peggy has tried unsuccessfully many times over the years to wrest from his possession and quietly lose. A large thermos jug of good coffee stands on the table beside him, most of if destined to waste. After one cup, Alfred will be too deep in conversation to remember to pour more, either for himself or for his interviewers. One helps oneself while he talks on, occasionally pausing to light his pipe but too occupied to keep it going.

Cats are distributed about the room. They invest the interviewers' laps. None of them ever thinks of sitting on Alfred.

The distant sounds of the household mingle with the buzz of traffic on the road just beyond the hedge of the ancient garden. Without pausing to take thought in answer to any question, leaning forward to emphasize every point, grimacing and raising his eyebrows as far as they will go to express any form of outrage or wonderment, Alfred Deller talks.

DELLER: There's a widely held opinion that the countertenor is an essentially English voice. This isn't true. It was, in fact, a European voice. There is a good deal of evidence to support the view that if it is not the oldest known voice type, it is *one* of the oldest; and we find composers in several countries writing for it as far back as the thirteenth century, in ensemble and as a solo voice. Later, of course, Bach employed countertenors as descant singers. Mind you, having said that, there's no doubt that England was the place where the voice was especially widely used and developed, particularly in the seventeenth century.

Q: But do you feel justified in singing Bach's alto arias? Are they really suited to the countertenor voice?

DELLER: The quick answer to that is that Bach would certainly have used boys, or students, never women; therefore, historically speaking, I don't see that there can be any objection. Then, I feel, the question of pitch becomes very relevant here. To be absolutely frank, as things are with the modern pitch, most of the Bach arias lie uncomfortably high for the countertenor. If we wish to hear the B minor Mass as Bach heard it we must perform it in A minor, at least a whole tone lower, because pitch has been going up and up since about 1860.

Q: Then, works which could be in your repertoire—and should be, historically speaking—have been taken out of your range by the rise in pitch?

DELLER: Yes. If the pitch were lowered by a whole

tone, everything that Bach wrote for the alto would be comfortably within my range. As it is, I can, and do, perform single arias out of context, because they can be transposed. For example, one of the first recordings I made for Vanguard, more or less as a fill-up, was the *Agnus Dei* from the B minor Mass. I've had letters from many parts of the world from people saying that this has given them a completely new conception of Bach. I think this is because of the particular ability of the countertenor voice to convey the religious sense of the work, and from the instrumental quality of the voice, especially in a slow-moving aria.

I remember Michael Tippett remarking on this when we first did the Bach Magnificat. There's a marvellous duet for alto and tenor, *Et Misericordia*; but you see, it's highish in the tenor and quite low for the contralto, and there is a problem to get a real matching. When the voices go one above the other and sometimes the alto goes below the tenor, then it's not a question of whether the contralto is any good, or not, but whether you can really get this intertwining of sounds and timbre between the two voices. With the countertenor replacing the alto you really can get it, because of this instrumental quality I'm speaking of. Out of the same work there's the *Esurientes* for alto, which pipes along with two flutes. The countertenor voice, having this same sort of fluty sound, answers the instruments ideally, while a female voice, however beautiful its quality, just doesn't match the quality of the instruments.

Q: Does the repertoire available to you fulfil all your needs?

DELLER: I think the whole literature from, shall we say, the thirteenth century right through to Bach and Handel offers music in plenty to express everything that I might wish to express. As to the nineteenth century, I've been absolutely firm since I started to sing as a professional to keep clear of all the composers of the romantic period, except for my own pleasure. They didn't conceive their music for anything like my type of voice, and it can never make their songs sound right. I love Schubert's songs, and when I was eighteen I won the *lieder* classes of two musical festivals in Kent with *Du bist die Ruh*. But I only did it because there was no special category for my kind of voice, and it was a case of sing Schubert or don't enter at all.

Q: But you have been prepared to perform works by modern composers who have written for you?

DELLER: Certainly. I'm interested that music should be written by contemporary composers for the countertenor voice, and I think it is possible to achieve good results. The obvious example is the marvellous part Britten wrote for me in *A Midsummer Night's Dream*. I have also sung interesting works in the modern idiom written for me by people like Michael Tippett, Edmund Rubbra, Wilfrid Mellers and Peter Racine Fricker, and Alan Ridout.

Q: In performing works of the thirteenth to seventeenth centuries, say, aren't you up against some difficulties not only of pitch, but of matching your voice to modern instruments?

DELLER: Very much so. Not only have most modern instrumentalists no conception of how to play down sufficiently to get a real sense of ensemble, but their instruments make it almost impossible to get a convincing balance. The works were simply not conceived for, shall we say, modern violins using wire strings and sound posts here and there to get the utmost resonance out of the instrument. Therefore, whenever the Consort records a major work, we try to ensure that it is in association with someone like the Concentus Musicus of Vienna, using original instruments. Then the whole thing takes on an entirely different aspect. There is no question here of trying to create atmosphere for its own sake, or achieve 'period' effects. The old instruments, by their very nature and size, and the fact that they have gut strings, and so on, can play with a convincing vitality of sound which really matches the voice. Moreover, they can do this and still play softly enough in an alto aria such as *A refiner's fire* in the *Messiah*, which a modern orchestra, however sympathetic, cannot play without losing that vitality.

As another example, when we performed the *Messiah* in the 1966 Stour Music with the Concentus Musicus, Maurice Bevan sang *The trumpet shall sound* not with a modern trumpet, but with a clarino, and there's no other word than ethereal for the result. Naturally, when your baritone sings that aria with a modern trumpet he feels he has to give his all to match the trumpet's sound. Now, at the first rehearsal, when we heard the clarino I said to Maurice, 'This is what Handel meant! "The trumpet shall sound"—not the martial sound of the military trumpet, on a human level of calling the forces together, but as a heavenly trumpet from afar, the still, small trumpet in the ear.' Maurice scaled down his performance accordingly; he didn't have to struggle at all, and the whole thing was a revelation.

Q: Surely, the ideal would be for the Deller Consort to have its own instrumental ensemble, with original instruments, working with it constantly in mutual understanding?

DELLER: Vocally, that is exactly why I formed the Consort. As to instrumentalists, nothing would give me greater delight, for example, than to get up here in the morning at Barton Cottage, eat a leisurely breakfast, then be able to say, 'Right, ladies and gentlemen, we'll work for an hour or two before lunch...' If one had all the money in the world, it would be quite easy to contrive, and it would be possible to make ideal performances of many wonderful works which the normal rush of engagements doesn't make it possible to study and rehearse. But money and organizational problems rule this out, and it isn't possible to team up, as it were, with any one existing instrumental ensemble, because all of them, like us, have their own engagements and travelling which would conflict too much. Fortunately, instead, we've been able to work on the Continent with such wonderful ensembles as the Scuola Cantorum Basiliensis, of Basle, the Capella Colloniensis, of Cologne, the Musica Antiqua, of Vienna, and, of course, the Concentus Musicus. In America, a lot of universities have extremely good collegium ensembles, with whom it's a pleasure to work.

Q: Is there an ideal accompaniment to your own voice?

DELLER: I think I enjoy singing to the lute more than anything else, not only because of the quality of its sound but because I have suffered so much from trying to get a balance when having to sing with any other instrument that has happened to be available.*

Q: Similarly, are there ideal performance conditions?

DELLER: Thank God, nothing takes the place of public performances. Believe me, it isn't just a question of wanting applause— though, of course, it's always pleasurable to hear lots of it and know that one is going across well. But for me, particularly, the music of the Renaissance, and so on, represents a sort of conversation between the artist and the audience. You've got to establish a *rapport* between you, and get to know one another quickly in order to do full justice to the music as artist and hearer. I would say that one knows, as an artist, within the first few minutes of beginning to perform whether that *rapport* exists already, or can be achieved by working at it, or won't be forthcoming at all. Generally, of course, a fairly small audience in intimate surroundings gives one the best

---

*Desmond Dupré commented: 'A harpsichord is perfectly all right for a slightly later using, and I think the voice and the instrument go together well. I think the lute has the advantage that the countertenor voice, certainly as used by Alfred, goes in more than any other for a lot of dynamic change, a great many dynamic nuances, which you can't get on a harpsichord satisfactorily. A piano can do it, but that doesn't really suit the voice, whereas a lute can do it and does suit the voice.'

chance. I reckon six or seven hundred, given the right hall and the right acoustic, is about ideal. But whether one is performing to a couple of hundred at Olantigh, or a couple of thousand in a town hall, it's the acoustic which really matters. For vocal ensemble music, we like it to be lively, not too dry—something with a bit of resonance. *

I've said something small with a few hundred people is ideal, but we've had some surprises in our travels. I think of that vast hall in the University of Iowa, which must seat two thousand comfortably, where Desmond Dupré, Robert Conant and I performed some years ago, just raised on a platform in this vast arena—and they said every single note was audible at the back. Then there's the Sydney Town Hall. It seems as big as Euston Station when you've got to sing in it. We had an audience of eighteen hundred and I believe they heard every note.

Q: You're sensitive about the way you're treated after the performance, as well as during it. Is there an ideal form of hospitality which concert organizers might do well to copy?

DELLER: Artists vary, of course, but for my part, and the Consort's—and I think a lot of others would agree—the immediate need is to unwind a bit, to recover. You can't do this if you're thrust into the middle of a throng, even if it's an admiring one, and expected to meet people and talk. What

---

*One of Alfred's anecdotes concerned the aristocratic organizer of a stately home concert who, when told the acoustic was rather dry, replied, 'How tiresome. Shall I spray it?'

we like best is to be shown to a table in some other room at which we can sit down and have a few quiet drinks and something to eat. Then one joins the party afterwards feeling fully able to do so, and I think both sides get more pleasure from it as a result.

Q: You've been speaking of the ordinary listener's response to you: now, what about the professionals in the audience—the critics, the musicologists? Does their presence inhibit you at all?

DELLER: It used to a little, but not now. One can only do one's best as one conceives it, and hope to be criticized without prejudice. As to musicologists, well, I tend to think of them as inhabiting two distinct worlds. There are those whose work I accept and appreciate—the ones who have done so much, particularly in recent years, to rediscover manuscripts and writings on music which have been extremely valuable to the practising musician. But there are the others who enter the realm of practical music, and then it can be very dangerous. To write intelligently on a musical subject—even, if you like, to discuss what pertains in the way of notation and give their views about stylistic indications—is one thing. To come between artists and their art is another. The tendency is to drain the music of any inherent life, and produce the type of performance which they refer to on the Continent as 'vegetarian music'. A German performer told me once that before the first rehearsal of a major Bach work in Munich the conductor addressed them all to the effect that, 'We want no sense of emotion in this work at all.'

Now, this is something I've been up against with musicologists myself. The basic thing with me, all the time, is that even if music was written four hundred years ago it was written by human beings for human beings; and human beings have not changed in our fundamental hungers, and desires, and emotions. Ninety per cent of the madrigal texts, for instance, are on the subject of unrequited love or on the joys of love fulfilled. In my opinion it is absolute nonsense to treat these marvellous works coldly: in which case, however beautifully they are played and sung, there will be no real personal communication through them. Unfortunately, these people who would de-vitalize such works are nothing if not industrious, and write for every possible publication, so that they have managed to influence for the worse the performance by well-meaning amateurs, if not by professionals, of a great deal of old music. No, I think musicology and the performance of music are two worlds best kept apart from one another.

Q: Apart from 'beware of musicologists!', have you any other advice for aspiring countertenors—indeed, for other singers?

DELLER: An important thing for a countertenor to bear in mind always is that there's nothing remarkable about being able to sing high. A lot of men can sing higher than I can. What matters is what one does with the voice, how one uses it, and this is something which cannot really be taught to anyone who can't experience it instinctively. There's a constant mistake on the part of young, enthusiastic countertenors to attempt things which are unnecessarily high, or, even when they're at liberty to transpose, to choose to sing at too high a *tessitura*. From the point of view of mechanics alone the voice must thin out as it goes higher, however well the notes are negotiated, so that there isn't the possibility of getting real resonance. Young singers say to me, 'Of course, in the morning I can take a top A', as though I am supposed to fall over backwards in admiration. I hasten to point out that it isn't necessary at all: if they would put their songs down lower, they would develop much more resonance in the voice. The most important thing for all singers, I believe, is an understanding, and an acceptance, and a humility in the presence of what Nature has given you. As I see it, in providing you with a voice of one type or another, Nature has given you a frame of certain dimensions. You've been handed the frame: now, you have to fill in the space it encloses; and you achieve much of this by hard work. But, by the mystery of God, every voice, even a great voice, has been given a frame of specific dimensions, and there's nothing to be gained by trying to alter it. It's no use saying, 'I'm a lyric tenor, but I'm going to become a dramatic tenor, because I want to sing Wagner.' I'm afraid this does happen. There are those sopranos with beautiful mezzo voices, straining away at trying to become dramatic opera singers until their voices become shrill and full of vibrato and out of context. Unless one faces up to making the most of what one has been given, and not trying to kick against the pricks, one won't achieve anything. This applies perhaps even more so to counter-tenors, who should, in my opinion, be very careful to confine themselves to the music written for the voice and not try to embark on things which were never intended for the male alto to sing.

Q: You've filled in the frame of your art as fully as one can conceive of its being done. Yet, you seem to feel that if life, like art, has its God-given frame, you have somehow failed to fill yours completely. What more do you think you could possibly have done?

DELLER: I think, as I said, that there has been something lacking in the way of human relationships; though, in my defence, I must repeat that this has sprung from what is basically a deep shyness on my part which some people have read incorrectly as a sense of my own superiority and importance. We're all guilty of this too often in life. We meet someone and too easily form some impression of them, come to a conclusion about them, and only when we get to know them really well do we find it completely disproved. One of the most important things in our relationship with our fellow beings seems to me to be to remember that things are seldom what they seem in any of us. My other fundamental regret, perhaps, is this feeling of not having done enough for those people whom my art doesn't reach.

Q: This feeling that you should be visiting the sick, and so forth: to be honest, if you had the leisure, would you really do it?

DELLER: I'm afraid not. I know that I am one of those one-track people, and that my life is music and nothing outside it.

Q: In saying that, are you perhaps indulging in a convenient kind of escapism—using it as a good excuse for not facing up to the bigger issues?

DELLER: I may be. But, genuinely, for good or ill, music is the one thing in my life. Perhaps if music had left me, and I'd been given the leisure you speak of, I might have managed to do something with it. But I can't conceive of that. I can't conceive of life without music, and I believe that, if it did stop, I would be unable to do anything else. It's the one thing that gives meaning to my existence—my work, my music. Everything stems from it. Everything.

ALFRED DELLER: Complete Discography

Alfred Deller's legacy on record goes back to the time of the 78s, with the first records issued by HMV and, as regards most of them, ultimately transferred to 33 r.p.m.

Then followed recordings made for Decca (L'Oiseau Lyre), Deutsche Grammophon Gesellschaft (Archiv Series), O.R.T.F. (France) and Deutsche Harmonia Mundi, and last but not least, the impressive collection realised by Vanguard (U.S.A.) and made available in Europe by Amadeo (Austria) or Phillips-Fontana.

For the last ten years the records have been made by Deller Recordings, in association with Harmonia Mundi France.

This discography aims to be complete. In most cases the records are described by their original reference. Whenever possible, present availability is indicated.

(Discography established by Alan Howlett)

VANGUARD U.S.A.

TR 5008 (45 RPM)	PURCELL	Music for a while/The fatal hour.
VRS 479	ENGLISH FOLK SONGS	(The Three Ravens).
(Available as VANGUARD 5-299E)		
VRS 1001	Wraggle Taggle Gypsies.	
VRS 1031/VSD 2014	Western Wind.	
(Available as VANGUARD 73005)		
VRS 1073	The Cruel Mother	
VRS 1055/VSD 2058	VAUGHAN WILLIAMS	
VRS 499	Holly and Ivy.	
VRS 1062/VSD 2078	Hark, ye Shepherds.	
BG 654/BGS 5066	Carols and Motets for Nativity.	
SRV 141/SRV 141SD	Album of Beloved Songs.	
BG 680/BGS 70680	Carols and Motets of Mediaeval Europe.	
(Available as BACH 70680)		
BG 570/1	HOMAGE TO PURCELL.	
BG 559	PURCELL	Ode for Saint Cecilia's
(Available as VANGUARD HM 33)		Day.
BG 590/BGS 5015	PURCELL	Welcome to all pleasures/ BLOW. Ode.
BG 547	PURCELL/JENKINS/LOCKE.	
BG 561	TAVERN SONGS Vol. I	

BG 602/BGS 5030	TAVERN SONGS Vol. II	
BG 635/BGS 5047	PURCELL.	Come, ye Sons of Art.
(Available as VANGUARD HM 14)		
BG 664/BGS 70664	PURCELL	Dido and Aeneas
BG 682/BGS 70682	PURCELL	The Masque of Diocletian.
(Available as VANGUARD HM 13)		
BG 622/BGS 5045	MACHAUT	Notre Dame Mass/
(Available as VANGUARD HM 1)		PEROTIN.
BG 656/BGS 70656	FRENCH MEDIAEVAL MUSIC	
(Available as VANGUARD S298)		
BG 604/BGS 5031°	MADRIGAL MASTERPIECES Vol. I	
BG 639/BGS 5051°	MADRIGAL MASTERPIECES Vol. II	
(Available as 2 BACH 5031–5051)		
BG 565	ITALIAN SONGS	
BG 567	MONTEVERDI	Il Ballo delle Ingrate.
BG 579/BGS 5007	MONTEVERDI	Madrigali Amorosi (8th
(Available as VANGUARD HM 10)		Book)
BG 612/BGS 5038	DELLER'S CHOICE	
BG 640/BGS 5052	LALANDE	De Profundis.
BG 613/BGS 5039	COUPERIN	Lecons de Tenebres.
BG 550	BACH	Cantatas Nos. 54/170
BG 601/BGS 5029	HANDEL CONNOISSEURS	
BG 661/BGS 70661	HANDEL	Queen Anne Birthday Ode/Anthems
BG 666/BGS 70666	HANDEL	Alexander's Feast.
BG 671/BGS 70671	MONTEVERDI	Lamento d'Arianna/
(Available as VANGUARD S 297)		Madrigals.
BG 691/BGS 70691	DUETS FOR COUNTER-TENORS (with Mark Deller).	
(Available as VANGUARD C 10022)		
BG 551	TALLIS	Lamentations of
(Available as VANGUARD S 287E)		Jeremiah.
BG 539	ELIZABETHAN AND JACOBEAN PIECES	
(Available as VANGUARD S 306)		
BG 576	ENGLISH LUTE SONGS	
BG 606	MUSICAL PANORAMA OF SHAKESPEAREAN ENGLAND.	
BG 553†	ENGLISH MADRIGAL SCHOOL Vol. I	
BG 554†	ENGLISH MADRIGAL SCHOOL Vol. II	
(†Available as VANGUARD 57/58)		
BG 577†/BGS 5002	ENGLISH MADRIGAL SCHOOL Vol. III	
BG 578*	ENGLISH MADRIGAL SCHOOL Vol. IV	
BG 624	The Silver Swan	
BG 563	The Cries of London	
BG 557	William Byrd and His Age.	
SRV 157/SRV 157SD	MORLEY/WILBYE.	Madrigals
(Available as VANGUARD HM 4)		
BG 673/BGS 70673	DOWLAND	Awake, sweet dove.

ALSO AVAILABLE ON VANGUARD

VANGUARD HM 6	BYRD	Mass in 3 parts/Mass in 4 parts.
VANGUARD HM 7	BYRD	Mass in 5 parts/Motets.
VANGUARD HM 47/8	THE ART OF ORNAMENTATION AND	

or 2 BACH 70697/8   EMBELLISHMENT.
VSD 729/30   THE ART OF ALFRED DELLER.

HARMONIA MUNDI FRANCE

HM 201 (AVAILABLE)	BLOW	Odes.
HM 202 (AVAILABLE)	SHAKESPEARE SONGS	
HM 203 (AVAILABLE)	GESUALDO	Sacrae Cantiones/ Madrigals.
HM 204	Consortiana.	
HM 205 (AVAILABLE)	ENGLISH MADRIGALS AND SONGS.	
HM 206	MUSIC FOR CHRISTMAS	
HM 207 (AVAILABLE)	PURCELL	Te Deum/In Guilty Night.
HM 208 (AVAILABLE)	TALLIS	Lamentations of Jeremiah.
HM 209 (AVAILABLE)	MONTEVERDI	Tirsi e Clori/Madrigals.
HM 210 (AVAILABLE)	COUPERIN	Lecons de Tenebres.
HM 211 (AVAILABLE)	BYRD	Mass for 3 Voices/Motets.
HM 212 (AVAILABLE)	BYRD	Mass for 4 Voices/Motets.
HM 213	BYRD	Mass for 5 Voices/Motets.
HM 211/213 (AVAILABLE)	BYRD	The Three Masses/ Motets.
HM 214 (AVAILABLE)	PURCELL	Ayres. Vol. I
HM 215 (AVAILABLE)	DELLER SOLO.	Vol. I
HM 216/7 (AVAILABLE)	HANDEL	Acis and Galatea.
HM 218 (AVAILABLE)	PURCELL	Ayres. Vol. II
HM 219 (AVAILABLE)	GIBBONS	Madrigals, Sacred Pieces, Fantasies.
HM 220	GESUALDO	Sacrae Cantiones. Vol. I
HM 221 (AVAILABLE)	MONTEVERDI	Mass for Four Voices/ FRESCOBALDI
HM 222 (AVAILABLE)	PURCELL	Queen Mary—Ode/Saint Cecilia—Ode
HM 223 (AVAILABLE)	TUDOR MUSIC	
HM 224 (AVAILABLE)	WEELKES	Cries of London
HM 225 (AVAILABLE)	MUSIC FOR THE ENGLISH CATHEDRALS	
HM 226 (AVAILABLE)	FOLK SONGS	
HM 228 (AVAILABLE)	DELLER SOLO. Vol. II	
HM 230	GESUALDO	Sacrae Cantiones. Vol. II
HM 231 (AVAILABLE)	PURCELL	The Fairy Queen
HM 232 (AVAILABLE)	TOMKINS	Sacred Pieces/Madrigals
HM 233 (AVAILABLE)	PURCELL	Verse Anthems
HM 234 (AVAILABLE)	GREGORIAN CHANT	Vol. I
HM 235 (AVAILABLE)	GREGORIAN CHANT	Vol. II
HM 236 (AVAILABLE)	GREGORIAN CHANT	Vol. III
HM 237 (AVAILABLE)	GREGORIAN CHANT	Vol. IV
HM 238 (AVAILABLE)	GREGORIAN CHANT	Vol. V
HM 239 (AVAILABLE)	GREGORIAN CHANT	Vol. VI
HM 240	GESUALDO	Sacrae Cantiones. Vol. III
HM 241 (AVAILABLE)	MORLEY	Triumphs of Oriana
HM 242 (AVAILABLE)	PURCELL	Catches/Laudate Ceciliam
HM 243 (AVAILABLE)	PURCELL	Indian Queen
HM 244/6 (AVAILABLE)	DOWLAND	Lute Songs/Lute Solos/ Consort Music.

HM 247 (AVAILABLE)	PURCELL	O Solitude/Anthems.
HM 248 (AVAILABLE)	GREGORIAN CHANT	Vol. VII
HM 249 (AVAILABLE)	PURCELL	Music for a while/etc....
HM 250	GESUALDO	Sacrae Cantiones Vol. IV
HM 252/3 (AVAILABLE)	PURCELL	King Arthur
HM 260 (AVAILABLE)	THE ENGLISH RENAISSANCE.	

(Some of the above have been reissued under the Harmonia Mundi label Musique d'Abord)

H.M.V. England

Early 78s		Most Deller/Bergmann discs have been re-mastered for L.P. and appear on Vanguard 'Homage to Henry Purcell', except:
C 4247	PURCELL	Retired from any mortal sight. Thus to a ripe, consenting maid (Old Batchelor) Hark, how all things (Fairy Queen)
7EP 7068	PURCELL	Music for a while/If music be the food of love/Thus to a ripe, consenting maid/Hark, how all things. (with organ works. Thurston Dart).
C 3951	DOWLAND	In darkness let me dwell/ Fine knacks
C 4178	DOWLAND	Sorrow stay/It fell on a Summer's day/What then is love but mourning.
C 4236	DOWLAND	Flow my tears/ANON. Caleno Casturame/ HUMFREY. Hymne to God the Father/ PURCELL. Evening Hymn.
C 4222	HANDEL	O, Thou that tellest (Messiah)/Alma de Gran Pompeo (Giulio Cesare)
B 10682	HANDEL	He was despised (Messiah)

Transferred to 33 RPM		
HLP 6	CICONIA	O Rosa Bella/ DUNSTABLE (Attrib.) O Rosa Bella
HLP 9	GABRIELI	In Ecclesiis
HLP 12	HUMFREY	Hear, O Heavens
HLP 14	PURCELL	What, what shall be done (excerpt)
ALP 1265	Shakespeare Songs and Lute Solos.	

DECCA. England

LXT 2798	ALDEBURGH FESTIVAL 1953.	
	PURCELL	O Grant the Queen a long life.
OL 50091-3	HANDEL	Sosarme.
(Available as OLS 124-6)		
OL 50101	BACH	Magnificat
(Available as OLS 127)		
OL 50102	CAMPION/BUXTEHUDE	
(Available as OLS 109)		
OL 50106	LULLY	Miserere/PURCELL.
(Available as OLS 102)		Come, ye Sons of Art.
DL 53003	LULLY	Misere.
DL 53005	PURCELL	Come, ye Sons of Art.
SET/MET 338-40	BRITTEN	Midsummer Night's
(Available as SET 338-40)		Dream.

DEUTSCHE GRAMMOPHON GESELLSCHAFT: Archiv. Germany

APM 14056	GIBBONS	Anthems, Madrigals and Fantasies.

CONCERT HALL

SMSC 2518AB	MONTEVERDI	Vespers. 1610
SMSC 2467	The Golden Age of English Music	

HARMONIA MUNDI. Germany

HM 17068	PRIMAVERA	
HM 17016	MITTELALTERLICHE WEIHNACHT.	
HMS 30823	MUSIK AN NOTRE DAME 1200.	
(Available as IC 065-99634	PEROTINUS	
IC 065-99718	MACHAUT/PEROTINUS	
HM 30628/9	VECCHI	L'Amfiparnaso.
(Available as IC 065-99816)		(Without spoken words.)
HM 17070	DIE SEEMANNSBRAUT	
	BYRD	Mass for 5 Voices/Motets.
(Available as IC 065-99815)		

ALFRED DELLER

A Singularity
of Voice

Alfred Deller (1912-1979) was more than a
singer: he was a musical experience. As with
many new experiences, it was at first hearing
somewhat of a shock when, from his great
frame and masculine presence, there issued
high, flute-like sounds, ranging effortlessly
the register of the female alto, yet
unmistakably male in character.

Until the advent of Deller the art of the
countertenor – a male alto of exceptional range
and flexibility – had been lost since the 17th
century. Because of this a vast quantity of
Elizabethan music, and that of England's
greatest composer, Purcell, who was also a
countertenor, had been completely neglected.
It was Alfred Deller who introduced it to
modern audiences, for whom it has proved a
refreshing and inspiriting discovery, and in the
process did so much to prove to other nations
that England is far from being 'a land without
music'.

Alfred Deller had strong elements of the
Elizabethan in him: a blend of artistic
sensibility, religious preoccupation, brooding
melancholy, yet infectious gaiety, which is
admirably brought out in this authoritative
and often amusing biography, extended and
revised from the original version, published in
1968 and long sought after in vain by Deller
enthusiasts all over the world.